VOLUNTEER ENCOURAGEMENT, ACCOUNTABILITY, AND EVALUATION

Marlene Wilson, Author and General Editor

Group's Volunteer Leadership Series™
Volume 6
Group's Church Volunteer Central™

Loveland, Colorado

Group's Volunteer Leadership Series™, Volume 6

Volunteer Encouragement, Accountability, and Evaluation

Copyright © 2004 Group Publishing, Inc.

Visit our Web site: **www.grouppublishing.com**

Credits
Author: Marlene Wilson
Editor: Mikal Keefer
General Editor: Marlene Wilson
Chief Creative Officer: Joani Schultz
Art Director: Nathan Hindman
Cover Designer: Jeff Storm
Production Manager: Peggy Naylor

Produced with the assistance of The Livingstone Corporation (www.LivingstoneCorp.com). Project staff includes Chris Hudson, Ashley Taylor, Mary Horner Collins, Joel Bartlett, Cheryl Dunlop, Mary Larsen, and Rosalie Krusemark.

Library of Congress Cataloging-in-Publication Data

Wilson, Marlene.
Volunteer encouragement, accountability, and evaluation / Marlene Wilson.—
    1st American hardbound ed.
    p. cm. — (Group's volunteer leadership series ; v. 6)
    Includes bibliographical references.
    ISBN 0-7644-2750-4 (alk. paper)
    1. Voluntarism—Religious aspects—Christianity. 2. Christian leadership. 3. Church work. 4. Voluntarism—Evaluation. I. Title. II. Series.
BR115.V64W555 2003
253'.7—dc22   2003022123

10 9 8 7 6 5 4 3 2 1   12 11 10 09 08 07 06 05 04

Printed in the United States of America.

Contents

Introduction

Because you are leading volunteers (or soon will be), I'm guessing that you have been a volunteer yourself. In fact, you may be volunteering right now as you create or revitalize your church's volunteer ministry.

We volunteers know the secret: When we have a volunteer job we're prepared to do, and we have all the materials and information we need to be successful in doing that job, it's *fun*.

Not only do we *enjoy* volunteering, we *delight* in it. It's fulfilling and satisfying.

Each of the volunteers serving in your church deserves to have a delightful experience. And here's the good news: You can make it happen!

In this last volume of the Volunteer Leadership Series, we'll focus on five more pieces of the volunteer leadership jigsaw puzzle. They're pieces you'll fit together to create delightful experiences for your volunteers . . .

Expectations often determine whether a person has a delightful, ho-hum, or poor volunteer experience. We'll look at how you can manage expectations in your volunteer ministry—your expectations and your volunteers' expectations, too.

Evaluation happens when volunteers find out how they're doing. This doesn't have to be a challenging time—if anything, it's a time of celebration! When it's handled correctly, an evaluation is something volunteers actually *enjoy*. I'll share with you how to set up the evaluation system so it's fun for you to give evaluations.

Accountability is expecting each person in the volunteer ministry to do what he or she agrees to do, and do it on time and with excellence. Here's practical help with building accountability into your ministry, and dealing with volunteers who are—and aren't—accountable.

Recognition of volunteers may become your favorite part of working with volunteers! Here are dozens of ideas for shining the spotlight on volunteers, honoring their service, and helping them feel good about their involvement.

Encouragement is like oxygen: Every volunteer needs it in abundance. We'll examine how you can create an atmosphere where encouragement is a natural part of your ministry culture.

Delight your volunteers and not only will you be serving them, you'll also go a long way toward keeping them on board as volunteers in the future, too.

Delight your volunteers. They'll delight you in return.

ONE
Expectations

**How to manage expectations in your volunteer ministry—
yours and those of your volunteers and leaders.**

Let me share a story with you . . .

My first year on staff at the Volunteer and Information Center in Boulder, Colorado, we did a pretty good job increasing the number of volunteers. But at the end of the year we realized there was a group we hadn't effectively involved: senior citizens.

We decided to form a task force, with the goal of getting more senior citizens on board as volunteers.

The first problem was that I didn't have a *clue* why seniors weren't volunteering. Were we doing something wrong? Was there something we weren't doing that we needed to do? I had no idea. I was totally in the dark.

The second problem was that I didn't have the slightest idea where to start building a task force.

I visited a senior center and told the director I was looking for someone to tell me what to do. I needed a person who was over 60 years old, was a good organizer, and who would give me free advice. The director said she'd see what she could do.

> "I didn't have the slightest idea where to start . . ."

Within a few days a woman by the name of Clara Clifford appeared in my office. She stood in front of my desk, crossed her arms, and said, "I hear you've got a problem."

I admitted she was right: I *did* have a problem. I needed to find someone who would tell me how to get seniors involved as community volunteers.

Clara pulled up a chair and sat down. She interviewed me for 90 minutes, probing to see what we'd done. She kept coming back to what my plans were for next steps.

"I don't *have* any next steps," I kept telling her. "I'm not sure *what* to do."

Finally Clara leaned back in her chair, sized me up, and said, "You're serious about this, aren't you?"

I confirmed I most certainly *was* serious. I'd just been subjected to an hour and a half of interrogation. How could I *not* be serious?

"Then I'll take it," Clara announced firmly.

> "She was told that her opinion mattered—but it didn't."

Here's the happy ending to that story: In one week Clara had 17 seniors on her task force.

Within a year she increased senior citizen involvement from 10 volunteers to 150 volunteers. The next year it rose to 250 volunteers. When it reached 350 seniors, I had to find more funding to keep the program from stalling out for lack of money.

Later, once Clara and I became friends, she explained what had happened in my office, why I'd been questioned with such intensity.

It seemed that Clara had served on a number of boards. She'd even reached state and national leadership in some of the organizations in which she served. But too often she'd been appointed to a position of authority only to discover that the current leaders didn't really want to hear what she had to say . . . or let her do significant work.

She was told that her opinion mattered—but it didn't.

She was told that she'd been heard—but nobody listened.

She was told that she would be given something important to do—but she wasn't.

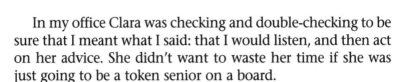

In my office Clara was checking and double-checking to be sure that I meant what I said: that I would listen, and then act on her advice. She didn't want to waste her time if she was just going to be a token senior on a board.

Clara wanted to make her expectations clear, . . . and to be sure I was clear about what I expected, too. In doing so, Clara showed tremendous wisdom.

Clear, expressed expectations are essential in volunteer ministry—and in life, too.

What Are Expectations?

Expectations are our assumptions about the future—how we anticipate things will go.

In a perfect world expectations are based on clear communication and agreements. But in the absence of those, people base their expectations on assumptions, implications, and wishful thinking. And that's a recipe for disappointment.

You see, what a person expects from a situation becomes that person's definition of what's reasonable and fair. And if others fail to meet those expectations, well, they're not being reasonable. Or fair. And they're certainly being a disappointment.

This principle operates *even if people never actually articulate their expectations*—to themselves or others! Expectations have the power to shade and interpret situations without ever making themselves known.

> "Expectations are our assumptions about the future—how we anticipate things will go."

Here's an example . . .

Suppose you receive a letter saying you've won the grand prize in a contest you don't even remember entering. Your name was drawn out of a hat and you're about to receive a check for a "substantial amount of money."

So you begin to plan what you'll do with the windfall. You'll give some to your church, some to your family, and with the rest maybe you can do some traveling. But where will you go? That depends on how large the check turns out to be. It's "substantial," but what does that mean?

Will you be able to book a vacation at Disneyland? Or better yet, Australia. And if you're in Australia, why not do it right with a two-week guided tour? And a stop-over in Hawaii to rest up, of course . . .

When the check finally arrives and you tear open the envelope, you find a thousand dollars and your heart sinks in disappointment. Substantial? They call *this* "substantial"?

Had the check arrived without your knowing it was coming, you'd have been delighted. You would have celebrated because it far exceeded your expectations. You thought you'd only find bills in the day's mail; instead there was a *thousand dollars*!

But because of your high expectations, now the check you received seems like pocket change. It won't finance your dream vacation. It doesn't feel fair. That's the power of expectations.

> **"That's the power of expectations."**

And make no mistake about it: Both volunteers and volunteer leaders have expectations about volunteer roles.

The Importance of Clear Expectations

Since we're expecting something from our volunteer experiences, let's take a tip from Clara and be clear about those expectations.

Here's where all your hard work will pay off. Because you have provided job descriptions and careful placement and you have helped set realistic expectations in the minds of your volunteers, they know exactly what they'll be doing. They know who they'll report to. They know how they'll be evaluated.

Of course, if you've not done those things, . . . well, it's not too late to do them. Without the clarity that comes with job descriptions, interviews, and careful placement, you'll struggle with unclear expectations regularly.

Clear expectations help both volunteers and volunteer leaders to have a realistic view of how the future will unfold, how tasks will be accomplished, and what the outcomes will be.

Before we move too far along, I'd like to share a quick word about expectations and volunteers. There are two general expectations that have proven to be true again and again in my decades of experience working with volunteers:

1. Volunteers want to do their best.

I've yet to meet a person who signed up to help in a classroom or at the food pantry with the intention of doing less than excellent work. Volunteers sign on the dotted line with every intention of meeting and exceeding your expectations. Many things can get in the way of their delivering an excellent effort (we'll discuss a few later), but it's safe to assume the best about your volunteers and interact with them accordingly. Volunteers are typically enthused, inspired, and happy to be on the team.

2. When volunteers fail to meet our expectations, it's not always the volunteer's fault.

As leaders, sometimes the problem is with us. *We* have failed to provide adequate information. *We* have assumed something that isn't true. *We* have not defined clearly what we expect.

If the problem lies with us, we can fix it. And if the problem lies with a volunteer, it's *also* our responsibility to proactively work to resolve it.

We may work directly with the volunteer or only with the person who supervises the volunteer, but we're likely to get involved. So let's talk about communicating clear expectations.

> "If the problem lies with us, we can fix it."

Clear Expectations Require Clear Communication

Again, if you've worked through all the steps described in this Volunteer Leadership Series, you've probably already established many clear expectations for volunteers.

But there are still things you will need to explain—and

have explained to you. Remember that volunteers are your *partners* in ministry; they have many valuable lessons to teach you, too. Communication is a two-way street.

Your ability to communicate clearly will help you in every aspect of handling expectations. Communicating clearly will help volunteers know what *you* expect. Your skills as a listener will help volunteers let you know what *they* expect. Clear communication helps everyone win.

> "Clear communication helps everyone win."

I've spent my entire career as a leader in volunteer ministries and agencies learning to communicate clearly, and I *know* I still have things to learn.

But here are three things I *have* learned again and again. I want to share them with you because they're fundamental truths about communicating clearly with volunteers. Owning and integrating these three truths into your own approach with people will help you manage expectations.

1. Everything you do communicates.

You can't *not* communicate. Even silence communicates something.

Here's an example . . .

Let's say you have a disagreement with a friend. Later you call and leave a message saying you'd like a return call so you can discuss the issue further and reach an agreement.

If several days pass and you haven't heard anything, you may call and leave another message. Then if a few more days pass without a return call, you may become angry or worried.

Is your friend ignoring you? Is your friend so angry he can't tolerate the idea of speaking with you? Is your friendship over? Or is your friend unable to phone back because he's ill? Should you call hospitals, or phone a mutual friend who can confirm your friend is still alive?

Notice: *Your friend is communicating with you even though he hasn't said a thing.* His silence is speaking—but you don't know what it means and may very well assume the worst.

You're communicating all the time—like it or not.

Interpersonal communication includes both content and emotion. The tone of your voice and your body language speak loudly about what's really being said. If your emotion and content are inconsistent, then the message is apt to be scrambled.

> "You're communicating all the time— like it or not."

And for some reason, scrambled messages *always* take on the most sinister, negative meaning possible. It's a phenomenon that defies the law of averages, like dropping buttered pieces of toast (they always somehow land butter side down!).

For example, suppose you congratulate a volunteer on a job well done. You say "Great job!" as you hurry past the volunteer in the church hallway. You look preoccupied and distracted (you're rushing to a meeting, so your mind is partially elsewhere), and you don't make eye contact. You don't give the volunteer time to respond. You deliver a "hit and run" affirmation that's sincere, but half-hearted. The result is a dual message: "I'm pleased—but not really."

Because your body language wasn't consistent with your words, the volunteer has to choose: Does she believe the words, or the actions?

I'm willing to bet she'll believe the actions.

It's easy to forget that we communicate in so many ways . . .

- Through touch—a tap on the shoulder or hug, a pat on the back or handshake. They all have strong meaning to both sender and receiver. When you touch, touch carefully and appropriately.

- Through visible movement—pointing a finger, winking, smiling, scowling, folding our arms. These communicate volumes without using a word, and often speak "louder" than the words we use.

- Through words and other audible symbols—including speaking, crying, and laughing, or a combination of these. Even a snort can imply that you don't agree with what has just been said to you.

• Through written symbols—in words, graphs, or even pictures. It's easy to be misunderstood when you send letters or e-mails, so be cautious. A rule of thumb: If what you need to communicate is corrective or confrontational, don't write it. Meet face to face, or at least talk voice to voice. Words are so easy to misunderstand.

2. Speak the truth in love.
In Ephesians 4:15 we read:

> *Instead, speaking the truth in love, we will in all things grow up into him who is the Head, that is, Christ.*

That biblical admonition requires that we be both truthful and loving at the same time. It's a hard balance to maintain.

When we strike this balance we speak directly and clearly, and get to the point. We don't gloss over issues. We don't adopt the conflict resolution strategy too many volunteer managers embrace: They *ignore* a problematic volunteer, hoping he or she will simply go away.

Speaking the truth in love requires us to take into account the words, feelings, and body language of the other person in the conversation. We must be present and caring even if we're unhappy. There's no room for blasting a volunteer for a mistake or using sarcasm in any way, shape, or form.

> "Straight, clear communication is exceedingly rare in the world."

Speaking the truth in love demands that we be clear about what we want— our expectations—and that we hear the expectations of others.

This sort of straight, clear communication is exceedingly rare in the world, and, sadly, in the church. But it's healthy and helpful. It spares volunteers sleepless nights as they try to interpret what we want, hope for, or envision based on our subtle insinuations.

When you speak the truth in love, so much can happen that's positive. It's worth learning this language of love.

3. Listening is communication, too.

I don't know who first observed this fact, but it's true. The world is full of good talkers but good listeners are so rare they're practically an endangered species.

I've been told the average talker speaks at a rate of about 175 words per minute, but the average listener can receive about 1,000 words per minute. Because of this tremendous gap, most people develop some very bad listening habits.

They let their attention drift to other things.

They assume they know where the talker is heading.

They use the time they're not paying attention to figure out how they'll respond—as soon as the talker stays quiet long enough to allow for a response.

But listening is more than just not talking.

A friend told me about a little boy who was in a music appreciation class. When he was asked to distinguish between *listening* and *hearing,* he replied, "Listening is wanting to hear." What a great definition! *That's* what listening is—"wanting to hear"!

> "Listening is more than just not talking."

We all say we want to hear, but it's not uncommon for us to miss the vast majority of what people say to us. Don't believe me? Outline the sermon you heard when you were last in church. How much of what your pastor said have you retained?

The challenge for us as leaders in volunteer ministry is to train ourselves to listen deeply. To hear not only what's on the surface but also to hear what is *beneath* the surface.

Our goal is to listen for the heart of what's being communicated. This requires that we pay attention to the whole person. As Jim stands before us, we "hear" his life situation as he brings it to our relationship. We hear his actions, his body language, his subtle emotional cues, his voice quality, his voice volume, his eye contact patterns, his unconscious gestures. When they're all on our radar screen, then we're really listening.

> "Our goal is to listen for the heart of what's being communicated."

We can do it—listening is a set of skills, not a rare gift that God has given to only an anointed few. I don't deny that listening is a complex process that can break down at any number of points and, if that happens, our expectations can get lost in the muddle. But the need to communicate clearly remains, and not just because it's the only way to be sure our expectations are being understood. It's also how we know that we are understanding the expectations of others.

And it's where we do ministry. Listening—heart-to-heart listening when we connect deeply with volunteers—is a gift to us both. When we move past discussing the weather to discussing how we feel about our faith, or the illness of our parents, or the pain we're feeling—that's ministry. We become open and truthful. We share who we really are.

There's no shortcut when it comes to clear communication. And there's no set of skills you can use that will give you a better return for your effort!

How Do You Set Expectations about Quality?

Just as volunteers want to do well in their volunteer roles, you, too, want the entire volunteer ministry to function well. We all want quality to be our hallmark.

But how do you get quality work from everyone in your ministry?

Here are some suggestions . . .

Communicate not just what work is to be done, but how it's to be done.

For instance, it's not enough for a volunteer to just show up on time to deliver a children's message. The volunteer must show up on time and be *prepared*, too. But what specifically makes a children's message a *quality* message? Is preparation enough . . . or is there more?

If supervisors of volunteers are providing excellent orientation and training, your volunteers will have a clear understanding of what quality looks and sounds like. But that happens only if volunteers' supervisors are consistent and clear. Be sure volunteer supervisors do an excellent job with orientation and training!

Ask: "What do you need from me that you're not getting?"

Ask every volunteer this question every three to six months. It gets at whether the volunteer's supervisor has a leadership style that's connecting effectively.

For instance, if Jane is a relatively "hands-off" supervisor and Shawn needs more guidance than Jane is providing,

"There's no short-cut when it comes to clear communication."

this question gives Shawn permission to ask for more help. This question also opens up discussions about training or materials that Shawn might feel he needs to be successful.

Ask: "What do you wish you knew about your volunteer job that you don't know now?"

Pose this question to each volunteer every three to six months, too. We want volunteers to feel comfortable in their jobs. If they answer this question by telling us they're unsure how to handle classroom discipline, or if they have a question about designing the church newsletter, we know we've got a problem.

Until volunteers feel adequately trained, they're likely to feel fearful or uncertain. This question gets at what your volunteers feel about their training.

If you regularly ask open-ended questions that are designed to solicit evaluations and probe areas where you can improve the volunteer ministry, then you'll find out if there's a problem with quality *before* the program begins to suffer.

Identify the problem that's interfering with quality and then set expectations for dealing with it.

Remember: Your volunteers want to see high quality, too. They're not out to deliberately disappoint you or the people they serve.

In my experience, the following three most common reasons for poor quality efforts from volunteers aren't all the fault of the volunteers at all. If anything, they can be traced back to us as leaders.

A lack of aptitude

At its core, this is usually the result of a volunteer being placed in the wrong position. Perhaps the placement interview didn't adequately reveal the volunteer's God-given abilities, skills, and passions. Maybe the volunteer didn't choose to reveal them in order to be placed in her current role—where she's failing.

This situation needn't end a volunteer's service to the church. Instead, simply place the volunteer in a new role that's more appropriate. There's no shame in failing to thrive in a position that's not in line with one's abilities, skills, and passion for ministry, but the volunteer may feel embarrassed anyway. Communicate your willingness to reassign the volunteer, and offer support in the transition.

Another alternative is to change the job so it fits the volunteer. Some positions are flexible enough to be easily adapted.

Communicate to the volunteer your expectation that things can't remain as they are; that change is needed. Then, with the cooperation of the volunteer, facilitate change.

A lack of skill

Picture a Sunday school teacher who loves children, loves teaching, and is ready and willing to lead a class every Sunday morning. Yet, this individual lacks the skill that comes with experience. Leave him alone with the fourth-grade boys more than 20 minutes and the room is reduced to charred rubble and chaos.

> "Look to redirect the volunteer to another role."

If there's aptitude but a lack of training, provide training. Use audio tapes, video tapes, provide books to read, identify workshops to attend. Even better, provide a mentor to come alongside the volunteer and help him grow in his skills.

If your best efforts to provide training still don't do the trick, look to redirect the volunteer to another role that's more in line with his or her current skills. This requires tact, but seldom is it a surprise when you tell a volunteer that things aren't working out. The volunteer already knows, and wants to resolve the situation somehow. Remember: Volunteers want to do well in their volunteer roles!

It's unfair to a volunteer to suggest that he or she is failing and yet be vague about the standards of excellence you require. "You're not good enough" is a message none of us like to hear. It's damaging, de-motivating, and seldom true. What *is* true is that the Sunday school teacher in question isn't able to maintain classroom discipline and create a learning environment.

Outline again what a well-disciplined classroom looks like, and help the volunteer see where there's room for growth. Jointly determine what will happen so the teacher can get the skills he needs. Then work the plan you've jointly agreed will do the job.

You've set fair expectations about quality because you've described what "quality" means in this context, and you've shown that it's possible to get there.

A lack of motivation

Sometimes it seems that a volunteer just doesn't care. A teacher no longer prepares adequately, a committee member skips meetings without explanation, a church treasurer lets checks and bills stack up.

Don't assume that a change in behavior necessarily signals a character flaw, or a total lack of concern. Rather than become offended, find out what the problem is and deal with it. If the volunteer reports directly to you, find out if the issue is your leadership style. If that's the problem, you can work to change how you relate to the volunteer.

> "Find out what the problem is and deal with it."

A volunteer may seem less reliable if there's a problem in the ministry area in which the volunteer serves. The group may be experiencing conflict, which often de-motivates volunteers. If that's the situation, deal with it.

A personal or professional problem may be consuming the volunteer's attention, leaving little time or energy to fulfill the volunteer role. Find out if it's a temporary or long-term issue; if it's the former, offer a short-term leave of absence and find out how you can support the volunteer through the crisis. If it's a longer-term concern, let the volunteer resign with your blessings rather than fade away.

> "Quality, like beauty, is in the eye of the beholder—until you define it."

And perhaps the volunteer just needs a reminder that what she does is important—and others are counting on her.

Quality, like beauty, is in the eye of the beholder—until you define it. If an expectation of quality is church attendance a minimum of three times per month, then say so. If the expectation is that they create lesson outlines a week in advance, be specific. You can't hold volunteers accountable to unexpressed expectations. Until you clearly communicate what you want, you're unlikely to see it.

When you see a lack of quality that isn't responding to your proactive involvement as the volunteer supervisor, be prepared to act.

Your people matter, but so do the ministry roles they're in. If the quality of a ministry program is suffering because of a particular person who can't or won't make the necessary changes to improve, prayerfully consider how to remove the volunteer.

But first focus on what *you* may be contributing to the situation.

In his book *The Five-Star Church*, Alan Nelson puts it this way, "Assume that you are part of the blame whenever quality does not take place. Perhaps it was poor communication or training."

Good advice. He goes on to share the risk of stopping there

without taking corrective action, "If you do nothing, . . . team members who are responding well can resent the lack of equity."[1]

> "Focus on what *you* may be contributing to the situation."

Don't get caught in the blame game, trying to determine exactly whose fault it is that a volunteer is failing to deliver quality after you've set clear expectations. Act—so the problem doesn't continue as you sort out who's responsible for what.

It's *essential* to confront problem situations. The first time a deadline is missed or a volunteer fails to show up for a scheduled event, deal with it. Make sure the unmet expectation is understood by everyone involved. There may be valid reasons why a commitment wasn't honored. But as a volunteer leader, you won't know until you raise the question.

And a word of caution: Don't try to "rescue" a failing volunteer by getting the staff (or other volunteers) to jump in and save the day. That action on your part sets an expectation, too, and may become standard procedure. You don't want to create that world, because you'll live in it.

Expectations aren't reality, but unless you are intentional about creating a culture where open, clear communication is what's normal, expectations may be as close to reality as anyone gets.

Attitudinal Blocks: When Your Expectations Aren't Met

Are you familiar with "attitudinal blocks?" Unfortunately, you probably are—and they can drain the fun out of running a volunteer ministry.

Think of attitudinal blocks as roadblocks on the way toward effective volunteer leadership. You're moving right along, expecting clear sailing, when suddenly you round a corner and smack straight into one. It can take your breath away and put you on the sidelines awhile.

You may never encounter the four attitudinal blocks I outline below, but many leaders of volunteer ministries do. I bring them to your attention for two reasons:

1. You'll know you're not alone if you encounter them, and

2. I don't want them to derail you as you move ahead in your ministry. Unmet expectations can do that to you.

> "It's *essential* to confront problem situations."

Don't think these problems are imaginary or far-fetched. The dramatic scenarios I describe below are based on actual situations. I present them as dramas so you can use them as role-play exercises in a small group or in a workshop for volunteer leaders.[2]

Attitudinal Block 1: You expect as the volunteer ministry leader to be considered a full member of the team—but you aren't.

Actors: Volunteer ministry leader, senior pastor, assistant pastor, and secretary

Setting: Church office

Volunteer leader: I'd find it helpful if we could set up a weekly meeting to get together and exchange information and concerns.

Assistant pastor: That's hard to do, since we're all operating on different schedules.

Senior pastor: Our schedules are constantly shifting. There isn't a time during the week we're even all here at the same time.

Secretary: I feel a need for an information-exchange meeting, too. I get telephone calls and sometimes don't know information people want. Maybe if we all got together, it would help me to get more lead time on information and be able to "plug in" better.

Assistant pastor: But you already do a great job keeping ahead of things, and we both update you at least once a day.

Senior pastor: The church doesn't work like other organizations. We're always on call. We can't just set up a weekly meeting and always make it work. We've tried before, but it's impossible to maintain.

Volunteer leader: I understand it'll be a challenge, but I still want to set a time for a weekly staff meeting, if only to help me. I feel responsible for the information being shared with me regarding needs and how church members want to help. At our meeting we could discuss how to best meet the needs of all our programs and people, and decide who would be best at dealing with them. I'd feel better if I knew we were following up effectively when someone wants to get involved in one of our ministries. I think we're letting lots of possible volunteers fall through the cracks.

Secretary: And I'd feel better if I knew everyone was being contacted. I feel bad whenever I type up the church directory and see names of people I haven't seen at church for a long time. Maybe they're being contacted, but if so, I don't hear about it.

Senior pastor: Well, I suppose we could *try* scheduling a standing meeting again and see how it works out. When do you suppose we could all meet?

They set a date, but the senior pastor then cancels because he later discovers he'd already booked that time for another meeting.

Attitudinal Block 2: You expect to be welcomed by the pastor, but instead you're perceived as a threat.

Actors: Pastor, lay leader
Setting: Pastor's office

Lay leader: I've been meaning to ask you, Pastor, how is our new volunteer coordinator doing? She's been on board here six months and I'm curious as to how it's working out.

Pastor: (hesitantly) Well . . . by and large, it's going very well. I mean she's very enthusiastic and a real achiever. She's getting things organized around here right and left! (Pause) But sometimes I'm afraid she goes a little bit overboard.

Lay leader: How so?

Pastor: Well, sometimes she strays into my domain. I mean our roles are still pretty fuzzy about who's supposed to do what.

Lay leader: That could get frustrating for both of you, I'm sure. Give me a "for instance" and maybe I can help.

Pastor: Well . . . several times she's actually gotten into doing *ministry* . . . and that's what I'm here for!

Lay leader: What kind of ministry are you talking about? Can you give me an example?

Pastor: Last week when Mrs. Peterson died so suddenly, the family called her to go talk to the Petersons' teenage daughter—and that was while I was still helping get things straightened out at the hospital. Why didn't they let me know the girl needed help—instead of calling her? After all, *I'm* the pastor here!

Lay leader: It sounds like you're angry about that.

Pastor: Of course I'm not! I'm just . . . well, I guess I *am* angry. *I've* been called to be the pastor. What do you expect me to do—just sit here and let her take charge? Her job description says *she's* responsible to *me.*

Lay leader: You mean she's not communicating with you?

Pastor: Oh, she does that fine. It's just that she's supposed to find volunteers, plug them into programs, and run that show. *I'm* supposed to do ministry. That's my job.

Lay leader: So, it's when she starts caring for people that you get upset.

Pastor: I just don't want the congregation to get confused. Pretty soon they won't know where to turn—to her or me.

Attitudinal Block 3: You expect current church leaders to enthusiastically embrace the volunteer ministry—and they don't.

Actors: Volunteer leader, secretary
Setting: Church office

Volunteer leader: Mary, do you have a minute? I've just got to talk to someone!

Secretary: Sure, come on in. The pastors are gone and it's quiet for the moment. What's on your mind?

Volunteer leader: It's last night's council meeting. I'm so frustrated, I'm ready to quit!

Secretary: What happened?

Volunteer leader: It's not what happened—it's what didn't happen . . . again! I asked for time on the agenda to report on the results of the one-to-one interviews we've been conducting with church members the last two months. I wanted to remind the committee chairpersons to call the people I've referred to them.

Secretary: Sounds great. What happened at the meeting that upset you?

Volunteer leader: First of all, I ended up last on the agenda again—even after the purchase of a new garden hose! It was 10:30 and I could tell everyone just wanted to get out of there and go home, but I plunged ahead anyhow.

I asked four committee chairpersons about how their follow-up calls were going and not *one* of them had contacted one referral. Not one! Matt said he's been too busy. Amy says she hates hearing "no." Dave said it's easier to do things himself. And Roxie said she always feels like she's begging when she calls people.

Mary, these people *want* to help. They *want* to be called! Here are these "pewsitters" everyone gripes about finally volunteering for committees, and no one calls them. It's ridiculous!

Secretary: I can see why you're upset!

Attitudinal Block 4: You expect that you've got things under control, but you discover there's room for improvement.

Actors: Pastor, volunteer leader (who's been in that role for three years), and three members of the volunteer ministry task force (who've just returned from a "Volunteerism in the Church" workshop they attended with the pastor and volunteer leader.)

Setting: Church office

Pastor: This is our first meeting since the workshop on volunteer ministries. I hope everyone is still as enthused as I am about the planning we did at the workshop.

Task force member 1: I sure am!

Task force member 2: Can't wait to try out some of those new ideas!

Task force member 3: It was terrific to rethink where we're going with our ministry and what's really possible.

Volunteer leader: You know, when I got back, I realized we're already doing most of it—they just had fancier terms for stuff I've been doing for a long time.

Pastor: You've got some great things in place, but it's always a good idea to take a look now and then to see if we can improve on a good thing.

Task force member 1: For instance, we've never done personal interviews with our people—we've relied on time and talent sheets and casual conversations. My hunch is we really don't know a lot of our people.

Volunteer leader: When you've worked with them as long as I have, you know them. I just haven't written it all down. But just ask me who is good at almost anything that needs doing and I can tell you in a minute. No sense making things more complicated than they have to be.

How Do You Solve These Attitudinal Blocks?

> "You can't mandate that attitudes change; you can only seek to understand."

I wish I knew.

The fact is there's no simple solution for becoming a fully accepted member on a team that's closed. Or for changing the attitude of a threatened pastor. Or for convincing church leaders that the volunteer ministry is valuable. Or, for that matter, overcoming resistance to change—our resistance, or other people's resistance.

What all these situations have in common is that they are, at heart, "people problems," and they have to do with expectations. They defy a quick, simple formula answer that fits all situations. Each attitude is personal, and flows out of someone's beliefs, experiences, and values.

You can't mandate that attitudes change; you can only seek to understand the people who hold those attitudes . . . and then work to change the attitudes by providing information and proven results.

When you're staring across a conference table at a row of disbelieving faces, it's hard to think the church board members will ever change their minds and will fund the volunteer ministry.

But they will.

When you see your pastor shake his head and tell you—yet again—that there's no way he'll approve your interviewing each church member about their abilities, skills, and passions, it's hard to believe that his heart can change.

> "You are on a mission that requires faithfulness and tenacity."

But it can.

You may be facing an uphill climb as you create an excellent, sustainable, thriving volunteer ministry. Maybe that's something you should have expected. To think something so valuable and precious could be birthed or taken to the next level without some childbirth pain isn't very realistic.

So set your expectations accordingly. Determine you'll be in the process for the long haul. Called by God and given a vision of your church that means being doers of God's Word as well as hearers of God's Word, you are on a mission that requires two things:

1. *Faithfulness*—to hear God and do what he tells you to do.

2. *Tenacity*—the decision not to give up.

Robert Greenleaf recounts a childhood story about a dogsled race in his hometown in his book, *Servant Leadership*.[3] Most of the boys in the race had big sleds and several dogs.

Greenleaf (only five years old) had a small sled and one little dog. The course was one mile staked out on the lake.

As the race started, the more powerful contenders quickly left Greenleaf behind. In fact, he hardly looked like he was in the race at all.

All went well until, about halfway around, the team that was second started to pass the team then in the lead. They came too close and the dogs got in a fight.

Pretty soon the other dog teams joined in, and little Greenleaf could see one big seething mass of kids, sleds, and dogs about half a mile away. So he gave them all wide berth, and was the only one who finished the race . . . which made him the winner.

> "If you are reasonably sure of your course— just keep going!"

As Geenleaf reflects on the gargantuan problems we sometimes face, he refers to that scene from long ago. He concludes:

"I draw the obvious moral. No matter how difficult the challenge or how impossible or hopeless the task may seem, if you are reasonably sure of your course—just keep going!"

And *that's* an expectation you can meet: never giving up.

1. Stan Toler and Alan Nelson, *The Five Star Church* (Ventura, Calif.: Regal Books, 1999), p. 93, quoted in Marlene Wilson, *The Effective Management of Volunteer Programs* (Boulder, Colo.: Volunteer Management Associates, 1976), p. 161.

2. This section about "attitudinal blocks" quotes heavily from Marlene Wilson's *How to Mobilize Church Volunteers* (Minneapolis, Minn.: Augsburg, 1983), pp. 77-83.

3. Robert K. Greenleaf, *Servant Leadership: A Journey into the Nature of Legitimate Power and Greatness* (New York/Ramsey/Toronto: Paulist Press, 1977), p. 14.

TWO
Evaluating Your Ministry

Make sure your volunteer ministry stays on target and is effective by using these evaluation tips and techniques.

Some things just naturally go together—apple pie and ice cream, fish and water. I'd like to suggest another natural pair—planning and evaluation.

In the context of your volunteer ministry, there are two general sorts of evaluations that you will do:

1. Evaluating the ministry itself.

2. Evaluating volunteers who serve in the program.

We'll get into evaluating volunteers themselves later in this volume, but for now let's walk through evaluating your volunteer ministry. It's essential to do this, and it's something that many volunteer ministry leaders never take time to do at all, let alone do consistently every six months or year.

Evaluating Your Volunteer Ministry

You really can't evaluate your volunteer ministry unless you've done thorough planning. As we begin a discussion on evaluation, I am assuming that you have become familiar with the process of planning and creating job descriptions we've shared in this Volunteer Leadership Series (see volume 3), and also that you are on your way to achieving both.

> "Planning and evaluation are tightly linked."

Planning and evaluation are tightly linked. You can't do a good job evaluating your ministry or your volunteers unless you've developed a mission statement and planned how to implement it, and you've created job descriptions for volunteers. Have you done all of those things? Great, because *the better you plan, the easier it will be to do evaluations.* After all, evaluation is simply deciding if where you've gone is, in fact, where you intended to go—how well you have followed your plans and implemented your goals.

You'll recall that in order for a *goal* to become an *objective,* it has to be specific, measurable, achievable, delegated, and move you toward fulfilling your mission statement. You probably struggled to create goals that fit all these criteria.

> "Did you do what you said you'd do?"

Well, it was worth the effort! Not only will those objectives you created help you do great ministry, but they will make it easy to do evaluation. Because they're measurable, you can tell if you succeeded in doing what you set out to do.

Did you do what you said you'd do? Did you do it on time? Within budget? And if not, did you . . .

- fail to delegate responsibility to someone to achieve the objective?

- not allow enough time or money for it?

- let other, newer priorities change your overall goals for the year, but forget to change your objectives and plans?

Remember, plans can change at any time. God may send you and your volunteer ministry off in a different direction, accomplishing your mission in a new way. That's God's privilege—but did you all agree that's what was happening? And did you change your action plans in writing?

Why Evaluation Matters

I'm a person most would probably describe as a "people person," and I'll bet you're one, too. That's why you're involved in a volunteer ministry—you enjoy people and love to help them grow.

So the idea of chaining yourself to a desk so you can crunch numbers and evaluate your ministry might seem like a waste of time. You'd rather be out helping volunteers be successful.

I understand—but it's still vitally important that you thoroughly evaluate your program on a regular basis. How else can you know if you're being effective, and demonstrate to your church leadership that the ministry is worthy of ongoing support?

Embrace the idea of evaluating your ministry. It may not be the favorite part of your job now, but it will help you know how to better serve and support your volunteers.

Maybe you think you're already doing a thorough job of evaluating your ministry. Let's briefly test that theory. Take the following test and see what you learn . . .

Are You Already Effectively Evaluating Your Ministry?

Use these sample questions to help you determine if there's room for more effective evaluation in your volunteer ministry.

Rate each of the eight areas based on this scale:
5 = Always; 4 = Regularly; 3 = Sometimes; 2 = Rarely; 1 = Never

___ We formally evaluate our volunteer program, analyzing our progress on the goals and objectives we have set for ourselves at least once per year.

___ We formally evaluate each volunteer to see whether he or she is accomplishing assigned tasks.

___ We talk with volunteers about their "job satisfaction," while listening carefully to their dreams, desires, wants, and needs regarding their work.

___ We provide an effective way for volunteers to give feedback to those people who are in charge.

___ We encourage volunteers to give feedback about how they perceive the quality of our ministry and the quality of their supervision.

___ When a new volunteer begins service, we hold orientation sessions.

___ When a volunteer leaves, we schedule and conduct an exit interview.

___ We contact a broad range of folks, within and outside of our program, to ask them to evaluate our effectiveness.

You have a possible score of 40 points. If you scored less than 35, you're missing significant opportunities to evaluate your program and volunteers, and to benefit from the feedback.

Myths about Evaluation

Evaluation is a tool you use to determine if your program—and the people in it—is doing what it's supposed to be doing. The evaluation process is as essential to the health of any volunteer ministry as is the planning process

Yet, evaluation is the tool most often neglected by church groups. Why? Probably because many of us have mistaken notions about what evaluation is and does. Let's examine and put to rest some of those myths.

Myth 1: We're not perfect, so evaluations are only going to hurt us by displaying all our flaws.

Fact: Evaluations, to be valid, must highlight both "well-dones" and "opportunities for improvement."

Example: At First Church, the people wanted to do a thorough evaluation of their volunteer-led food pantry. They braced themselves for lots of bad news about their budgeting, programming, personnel, and leadership, because the program had seemed to languish during the past winter.

Instead, they were pleasantly surprised by two facts that surfaced in the analysis: (a) A large new homeless shelter had been set up in a neighboring town, so that most of the hungry people in the area were now heading there for food and temporary lodging; (b) in spite of the new shelter, the church members discovered they'd been consistently feeding more people each year during the previous five years.

Their perceptions about the program had been flawed until the facts were uncovered.

Myth 2: Evaluations are purely statistical and boring.

Fact: Evaluations can be set up to record feelings, dreams, desires, visions, suggestions, and comments about what has happened—or what *should* happen. These can be more insightful and instructive than any statistics generated.

Example: After the vacation Bible school program at Second Church, informal survey forms were distributed to the teachers, parents, and children. The forms asked a few simple questions about what people liked, didn't like, and what they would suggest for improvement for the coming year.

The statements were printed up (anonymously) and distributed for everyone to read under two categories: strengths and weaknesses. Surprisingly, this was a very powerful and poignant experience for everyone. The "strengths" comments were heartwarming and encouraging. The "weaknessess" suggestions, for the most part, were right on target. And plans were made for realistic change. Later, most participants said: "What a positive experience!"

Myth 3: Evaluation is something done by specialists.

Fact: Rarely do churches hire professional consultants. In fact, most churches aren't "mega-sized" and therefore consultancy is ruled out. Instead, all participants involved in a project or program are invited into the evaluation process by the current leadership.

Example: After Joe had spent six months leading the Men's Retreat Planning Committee at Third Church, he was exhausted. Yet, because the retreat was such a success, he had a warm glow every time he thought about how his efforts contributed. Joe figured that glow was enough of a reward, so he was surprised when Pastor Smith set up an appointment with him and the rest of the committee members to evaluate how the process had gone for everybody. They all talked together, informally. They also filled out a Retreat Planning Feedback Questionnaire to analyze during a second meeting.

Joe and his committee members knew they had the skills to plan and produce the retreat. Clearly, Pastor Smith thought they had the skills to evaluate it as well.

Myth 4: Evaluation is an end in itself, a final report to wrap up a project.

Fact: Evaluations should help you decide what to add, drop, change, or keep. Program adjustment is the goal and chief benefit.

> "It's important to do both objective and subjective evaluations."

Example: At Fourth Church, the children's pastor did a complete organizational development process, surveying all aspects of children's programming. He helped the participants develop a mission statement, set goals and objectives, analyze and gather resources, and put plans into action.

A year later, when the evaluation process was completed, the leaders, volunteers, and parents decided to drop the high school "coffee shop" while adding a softball league for sixth through ninth graders. The evaluation process, in itself, was a tool for producing that change. Everyone knew there would be ongoing change and continual adjustment, because the new ministry configuration(s) would be evaluated annually.

Don't let believing these myths stop you from evaluating your ministry. They're myths—not accurate representations of evaluation or what it can offer you and your ministry.

Of all these myths, perhaps the one likeliest to stop volunteer ministry leaders from evaluating their programs (and volunteers) is the second myth: Evaluation is nothing more than stale, boring statistics.

Listen, it's important to do both objective *and* subjective evaluations to get an accurate picture of your ministry.

Consider the difference between the two . . .

Objective Evaluation

This type is simple if you've planned well. Just review all of your objectives for the year and determine whether your volunteer ministry accomplished what it set out to do—on time and within budget. If not, try to determine why. Then feed what you learn into next year's planning process.

The evaluation may reveal that you wrote a worthwhile objective but didn't allow enough time or didn't have the right person in charge. Or maybe you'll find that the need for a certain program no longer exists. Now you can drop or change that objective next year.

Subjective Evaluation

This type of evaluation is more difficult and rarely done in churches. Too bad, because a subjective evaluation is essential if you're going to be responsible for your people as well as your program.

You see, you've got to know whether your volunteers grew spiritually and as persons as a result of their involvement as volunteers. You need to know how they felt about the experience, whether their ideas were sought or ignored, and whether or not they received the support, training, and recognition they needed.

And did they feel they were truly in ministry?

These aren't small questions, and they reveal important information.

Dietrich Bonhoeffer was a mid-twentieth-century theologian and a martyr to the Nazis. In his book, *Life Together*, he suggested several questions any Christian community needs to ask to determine if the work it's doing is on target:

Has the fellowship served to make the individual free, strong, and mature, or has it made him weak and dependent? Has it taken him by the hand for awhile in order that he may learn to walk by himself, or has it made him uneasy and unsure?[1]

As a leader in your church's volunteer ministry, you need to know how participating in the ministry impacts people. Does it cause them to grow in their relationship with Jesus, or become a distraction to their spiritual growth?

You are involving Christians in ministry. You are helping your church do the work God has called it to do. You are cooperating with the purposes and plans God has for his people. It stands to reason, then, that the fruit of your efforts will be positive and good. But until you check through a thorough evaluation, you'll never know for certain.

The Three Big Questions

In my experience, there are three questions that must be part of your ministry evaluation:

1. What should we evaluate?

2. Who should do the evaluations?

3. What do we do with the evaluation results?

Let's examine these three questions in order . . .

Question #1: *What* Should We Evaluate?

It seems obvious to say, but you need to decide what elements of your ministry you want to evaluate. That decision will determine what tools (such as surveys and individual interviews) you'll need to gather relevant information, and to do a helpful analysis.

Again—if you've got solid goals and objectives in place, that's the place to start. They are designed to be specific, measurable standards that can be evaluated easily.

For instance:

- Did you recruit and place 25 teenage mentors in nine months?

- Did you set up three new food distribution centers, with four volunteers regularly scheduled to oversee each one?

- Did you implement a teacher-training program and graduate five new Sunday school teachers in the past quarter?

If you accomplished your objectives, then you can go on to ask: *How well is it working?* If you were able to accomplish an objective but it burned out half your volunteer staff to meet the deadline, there's a hidden problem. What looks like a success actually wasn't one—the cost was too high.

And if you *didn't* accomplish your objectives, you can ask: *What will we do about it—if anything?* Perhaps you could get those 25 teenage mentors if you recruit in two more high schools. Or maybe you want to abandon the mentoring program because you've discovered the liability insurance premiums for the program have doubled in price and you can no longer afford it.

It's challenging to evaluate a ministry. The elements of the program you choose to measure, the specific people you choose to interview—they all have a unique view of the program.

It's important that you move past general impressions and get down to hard numbers and real statistics. It's not that "soft" questions—the ones that call for judgment from the people being interviewed—are worthless. They're valuable! In fact, you must ask some questions that get at the reputation of your volunteer ministry. Here are some "soft" questions you might want to ask . . .

> "It's challenging to evaluate a ministry."

- Are volunteers enriching and extending paid staff efforts in achieving the purpose of the church, or are volunteers simply window dressing?

- Is the money expended on the volunteer ministry reasonable and justifiable when cost per volunteer is computed?

- Is the ministry accepted and supported by staff and administration? Do recipients of the ministry's efforts regard the ministry as valuable to them?

You can gain a world of insight by listening to the answers to these questions.

But you're also looking to discover quantifiable information. What can you measure and use as a yardstick from year to year to see if you're improving, static, or sliding backward in your effectiveness?

I'd suggest you find ways to measure the following items:

Time is a resource given by your volunteers, both individually and in groups. Find out how many hours have been given per week or month, or whatever time period you're evaluating. Use simple record sheets such as sign-in and sign-out sheets, or have volunteers report monthly how many hours they've given to the ministry.

Look for trends: Do you have more volunteers, but they're each giving fewer hours? Do you have some volunteers who give a great deal of time, and some that you seldom see? Are there more volunteers in the winter than in the summer, and how might you use that information in planning?

Turnover rate is a critical marker to track, too. How long does the typical volunteer stick with the ministry? Are there different turnover rates in different sorts of volunteer positions? If so, what does that tell you? What could you do to impact the average length of service among your volunteers? When volunteers consistently leave before the completion of their assignments or commitments, you've got a problem! Or when the average length of service remains only a few months, something needs changing.

Budget is a major concern. Are you under budget? Over? Right on the money? Is there a predictable time of year when the budget is tight or loose? What factors impact that? Which parts of your program seem to be marginal when you consider the "bang for the buck" factor? What might that information imply?

Achieving goals is perhaps the most obvious objective standard to check. Did you get things done you set out to do?

Question #2: *Who* Should Do Evaluations?

In the same way it was important to have key "affected individuals" represented in the planning process, it's important to have them in the evaluation process, too. These people should have a say in how the evaluation is conducted, and what is actually evaluated.

Affected people who should be represented in this process might include the volunteer manager, the volunteers, church staff, administration, and church members. All need to have the opportunity to evaluate the ministry from their perspective.

There are many tools that could be used to conduct the evaluation. However, because every volunteer ministry is unique, I strongly suggest that your task force drafts its own evaluation tool.

Don't worry—you don't have to start from scratch! There are denominations and other church groups that have created evaluation tools. If you have a denominational affiliation, check with your office. But one downside of using a denominational tool is that they're generally very specific to a single denomination; those tools don't translate well for use in every church.

> "You don't have to start from scratch!"

Let me outline the major issues you should include in your evaluation. Ask your task force to draft specific questions to fit under each heading.

1. Mission statement

Ask questions about whether the church's mission statement is effective, reviewed regularly, or needs to be adjusted. Ask the same questions about your volunteer ministry.

2. Volunteer ministry job descriptions

Ask questions about expectations, and the clarity and awareness of written job descriptions.

3. Identifying and interviewing volunteers

Ask questions about how volunteers are identified and interviewed in terms of their abilities, skills, passion, personality, and desire to serve.

4. Matching volunteers and ministry positions

Ask questions about how volunteer's abilities, skills, and passions are connected to church ministry needs.

5. Recruiting volunteers

Ask questions about interviewing, describing positions, offering choices; the entire volunteer recruitment process. And include questions about marketing the volunteer program, too.

6. Training volunteers

Ask questions about how effectively you're providing orientation, education, retreats, and training courses.

7. Supporting volunteers

Ask questions about how your ministry is encouraging, recognizing, and offering support to all your constituencies.

8. Completing a volunteer ministry assignment

Ask questions about what happens when a volunteer ends a project or term of office.

9. Evaluating the volunteer ministry as a program in the church

Ask questions about how the entire volunteer ministry is functioning as a ministry area of the church. What's your reputation? How effectively are you involved? Are you thriving and energized by the power sources discussed in volume 2 of this Volunteer Leadership Series?

The person directing the ministry should constantly conduct an ongoing, informal assessment. Feedback from staff and volunteers, observations, comments at meetings, volunteer reports, statistics and records—these all provide a picture of the ministry's ongoing health.

> **"Don't neglect periodic formal assessments!"**

But even if you are doing the job with such informal evaluations, please don't neglect periodic formal assessments! You'll find them useful as you prepare budgets and goals for the coming year. Use questionnaires and/or interviews with representatives from each of the groups affected by your volunteer ministry.

The person who directs the volunteer ministry needs to become a real fan of doing ongoing evaluations. Why? Because in the course of those evaluations the volunteer leader is

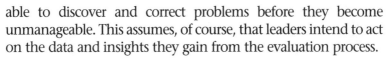

able to discover and correct problems before they become unmanageable. This assumes, of course, that leaders intend to act on the data and insights they gain from the evaluation process.

Question #3: *What* Do You Do with Evaluation Results?

Ivan Scheier answered this question well:

• Disseminate

• Discuss

• Do Something

• Don't File [2]

In other words, *act on results.*

May I suggest you carve that one in stone? Hang it on your office door where you'll see it often—as well as those who work with you in the volunteer ministry.

"You must act!"

You must act! Bring together representatives of all the groups involved in an evaluation and talk about what you've discovered. *But don't stop there.* Keep bringing your group together for the consequent re-planning and adjustment process.

This group will . . .

• Objectively examine the results.

• Explore alternative courses of action.

• Develop recommendations for improvement.

• Draw up a plan.

• Act on the plan.

A note: Don't forget all the good that's getting done! Be sure that in the course of discussion and planning the strengths of the program are recognized, reinforced, and celebrated.

Evaluation not only enables, but forces, us to examine the quality and value of our programs. Yes, we certainly want to know how to do the thing we do more effectively. But that's not enough. Let's also ask the hard questions about *why* we do them, and what happens as a result.

Exit Interviews

When you interview individuals who are leaving your program for some reason, it's not technically an evaluation of the volunteer ministry itself. But if you'll sift through exit interviews with an eye for trends, you'll get wonderful feedback about how your volunteer ministry is functioning. Exit interviews are used in many businesses because:

- The feedback about the company is often direct and clear; the employee is leaving and therefore more likely to be candid with comments.

- Who is better able to provide accurate feedback than someone who is familiar with the company, its policies and procedures, and its management?

Your church isn't a company, but the benefits of exit interviews are transferable. Don't miss this opportunity to find out how your ministry is doing, where you can improve, and where you're doing wonderful work already.

Set up the exit interview for *every* volunteer who leaves a position; don't reserve these interviews only for volunteers who leave while happy . . . or who are released from their positions. If you "cherry-pick" just people who are happy, you'll think everything is wonderful. If you consider only what disgruntled people say, you'll quickly become discouraged. Talk with everyone.

You might consider having someone other than yourself or the volunteer's supervisor conduct the interview. If there's a personality conflict, the volunteer might be more likely to reveal that information to someone else. You're looking for honest answers, so remove obstacles that might interfere with honesty.

> "Set up the exit interview for *every* volunteer who leaves."

My friend Betty Stallings has developed an exit interview for volunteer organizations you can easily adapt and use for your ministry.

Sample Volunteer Exit Survey Form

1. To what extent did you feel you reached the expectations listed in your job description? Share your reasons for any "gap" you perceive.

2. Was the time allowed to accomplish your volunteer work realistic? Explain your answer.

3. Did the church provide adequate orientation, training, supervision, and resources for you to accomplish your job? Comment, and offer suggestions for improvement.

4. What's been your greatest satisfaction on the job?

5. What's been your greatest disappointment on the job?

6. Were other volunteers and staff receptive and appreciative of your volunteer work? Explain your answer.

7. What were areas of growth in your volunteer job?

8. Overall, would you rank your performance as:
❑ Superior, exceeding expectations
❑ Excellent, you met expectations
❑ Needing improvement, you didn't meet expectations.
Explain why you chose the answer you chose . . .

9. What type of work and time commitment do you desire for next year? (Note: Only ask this if you would offer another position to the volunteer.)

10. Please share any other comments or suggestions.[3]

Courtesy of Betty Stallings

1. Dietrich Bonhoeffer, *Life Together* (New York: Harper and Row, 1954, 2003), p. 49, quoted in Marlene Wilson, *How to Mobilize Church Volunteers* (Minneapolis, Minn.: Augsburg, 1983), p. 66.

2. Ivan Scheier, quoted in Marlene Wilson, *The Effective Management of Volunteer Programs* (Boulder, Colo.: Volunteer Management Associates, 1976), p. 91.

3. Betty Stallings, "The Church and Its Volunteers" in the series *The Ministry of Volunteers* © 1979, Office of Church Life and Leadership, United Church of Christ. This was reprinted in its entirety, by permission, in Marlene Wilson, *The Effective Management of Volunteer Programs,* pp. 136-142.

Accountability: Your Part in Preventing Problems

Help for solving most volunteer-related problems before they happen, and four questions to ask when a problem does appear.

As you evaluate your ministry and your volunteers, you'll find opportunities to improve, to define problems, and then to do something to improve. That's the essence of accountability.

Nobody likes focusing solely on problems, but part of accountability is objectively examining problem areas and seeking to fix them. In these two chapters on accountability you'll see how that's done.

In this chapter we'll ask several important questions:

- Could the problem be the system?

- Could the problem be you?

- Could the problem be unresolved conflict?

- Could the problem be a difficult volunteer?

This final question is an important one, but I will deal with it fully in chapter 4.

Could the Problem Be the System?

Let me say again that working with volunteers is almost always a happy, fun, and rewarding experience. If you've been involved for any length of time, you already know this! And to keep your volunteer leadership experience on this high level of fulfillment and success, one particular attitude is crucial: When a problem arises, it's best not to immediately assume that an individual is at fault.

> "Working with volunteers is almost always a happy, fun, and rewarding experience."

That's right. Don't look to the individual volunteer first. Rather, look to the *system*—your policies and procedures, both official and unofficial.

I'm hoping you're already assuming the best of your volunteers and nurturing respectful, positive relationships on your team. With those attitudes in place you'll know that volunteers don't attempt to deliberately create difficulties; if anything, they go out of their way to *not* cause problems. When problems do arise, it's often the case that a change in the system or in the environment will bring everything back in line. You don't need a change in personnel.

But what, exactly, is a "system problem?" A little story here might help you visualize the phenomenon.

Imagine a company that produces widgets. It has two manufacturing plants, Plant A and Plant B, and at each location there's a hierarchy of managers. Plant A produces the widget and Plant B produces the packaging within which the widget will be shipped and displayed on store shelves.

All has been going well for years, until yesterday. Suddenly the packages are too small for the widgets! The vice president at Plant A picks up the phone and calls the vice president at Plant B. "What's going on with you guys over there?" he hollers. "The packages are too small! Here are the specifications we need . . . "

The conversation is brief; the crucial information is relayed. The packaging vice president then immediately calls his plant manager into the office. "What's wrong with you, Fred? The packages are too small. Check out these specifications!"

Fred hurries back to the plant and calls his foreman into the office. "Jake, are you nuts? You're really messing up here, and

I'm not going to stand for it. Look, these packages are too small."

Jake runs from the office and hustles over to Phil's package-sizing machine and yells: "Phil, look at your calibrations! They're off by a country mile!"

Phil says: "But I thought Geraldo, the widget-sizing guy over in Plant A, was now making a new, smaller widget! Boy, I guess I was wrong about that—and sorry about the loss of millions of dollars."

At this point, Jake realizes he has several choices. He can assume there's a personnel problem and fire Phil for incompetence. Or, he can go back and talk to his plant manager, who will talk to the vice president, who will call the other vice president over at Plant A. Then that vice president will talk to his plant manager, who will call his foremen, who will speak to Geraldo. And perhaps Geraldo will need to be fired, which should take care of the widget-sizing problem.

> "Adjust the system; solve the problem."

But Jake chooses a third alternative, a quick "system fix." He decides to install a phone next to Phil's machine so that Phil can talk to Geraldo about the widget sizes he's been instructed to produce. In fact, now the two workers can talk about specs and calibrations any time they want.

And guess what? For as long as Phil has access to that phone, there is never again a packaging problem!

That's just one example of how a system solution can be just what the doctor ordered when a program problem arises. Adjust the system; solve the problem.

There are countless possibilities for system problems, of course. So how could this type of thing occur in a church or other volunteer situation? Think about it . . . and test your creative problem-solving skills in a couple of possible scenarios—

Suppose . . .

Your Sunday school superintendent keeps forgetting to give you the attendance report after classes on Sunday mornings. Sometimes he lets you know as he passes you in the hall. At other times he calls later in the week and gives you a number. You, in turn, are either late or inaccurate in your reporting to the Christian education board. And you're getting pretty angry about that superintendent.

Your recommendations for a system change that could help . . .

_____

_____

_____

_____

(*A possible suggestion:* What if you both agreed to install a clipboard with attached pencil on the superintendent's wall? It could hold an attendance form ready for filling in, along with displaying your fax number, e-mail address, and phone number at the bottom of each page.)

Suppose . . .

Each day, after the kindergartners have their vacation Bible school snack time in the gym, there's at least one banana peel left on the floor. The custodian wants you to reprimand the teacher for being so incompetent.

Your recommendations for a system change that could help . . .

_____

_____

_____

_____

(*A possible suggestion:* Could you ask the teacher to stop serving bananas for snacks? Could the kids have their snacks outside? Or could a trash can be placed in the gym?)

Bottom line: Sometimes system problems are a quick fix, with few people involved. A few conversations, an update in your procedure manual, and it's over.

But sometimes they're at the heart of a large, far-reaching problem, and changing the system will require a significant amount of time and energy. Do it anyway—it's worth it.

When you sense that the system itself is your main problem, take these three actions—

1. Check the program evaluations you've done and see whether there are any holes. (Look for steps you may be skipping in the volunteer leadership system outlined in this series, or steps you aren't doing well.)

2. Set priorities, along with actions steps, for changing and improving the system. Make sure those priorities are communicated; you may not be the only one skipping steps!

3. Give yourself one to two years to do the fix or "plug the holes." Quick fixes are quick—but not always a fix. Take the time to do it right.

Could the Problem Be You?

Maybe you don't need to focus your concerns on the system at all. Maybe it's just a matter of looking in the mirror.

When the problem is you, it's usually because you aren't taking care of you. That is, maybe you aren't adequately

> "Quick fixes are quick—but not always a fix."

managing your own stress so you can more effectively manage the stresses among and within your volunteers. When leaders are stressed-out and maxed-out, ministries tend to experience more problems, and small wonder. The leaders don't have spiritual, emotional, and physical reserves deep enough to deal with issues that arise.

So consider your own life right now. Is it one of joy—or stress? Is it one that you'd like to maintain for a long period, or would you change it if you only knew how?

How's your stress level?

Most of us who are involved in church leadership can relate to hectic situations like these:

- The alarm didn't go off and you missed your 8:30 volunteer staff meeting.

- The senior pastor turned down that proposal you submitted three weeks ago.

- The church secretary was out sick, so you answered phones all day.

- You got stuck in a one-hour traffic jam on the way home from work.

As the pressure mounts, so does your blood pressure, and soon your head aches or your stomach hurts, you begin snapping at everyone (including strangers), your heart pounds, and you find yourself either becoming more aggressive or withdrawing into yourself.

> "Is your life one of joy— or stress?"

You're experiencing stress, and it's part of daily life for most of us. To be sure, a little stress isn't a problem. But when there's too much, or we are overwhelmed by it, stress can take a hefty toll. Stress has been linked with most major health problems, including heart disease, hypertension, ulcers, and cancer.

And like it or not, stress is no stranger in the church. As the leader of a volunteer ministry, you're responsible for the quality of work performed by people you don't pay and whom you may not directly supervise. That's stress!

You've got to learn to handle stress well for several reasons, not the least of which is that without mastering stress you'll never last long in a ministry position. You'll feel the joy and fun drain from your ministry; it will become drudgery you'd rather avoid.

Plus, when you handle stress well, problem situations tend

to gradually diminish—for reasons that have nothing to do with your volunteers or pastor.

Handling stress well can mean:

- **You don't overreact.** If you're overly stressed, you'll overreact to people and situations that appear to be problems. You'll treat small interruptions as major issues— because in truth the problem is you. You've got to understand and recognize when inner stress is fogging your vision and warping your assessment of others and the work they are doing.

> "Like it or not, stress is no stranger in the church."

- **You model stress-free volunteerism.** If you've learned how to recognize and manage your own stress levels, you can then model and teach those skills to your volunteers. It's amazing how many "problem people" can become ideal volunteers if their stresses are cared for. If they're nurtured and given hope, they can set about their tasks with renewed energy and positive spirits. It doesn't *always* work that way, of course. But isn't it worth trying to salvage those who, because of stress, are unhappy— and are making others unhappy?

Let's revisit those stressful scenarios I listed on page 50. There are three stressful components in each of them:

1. **The stressor**—the event or incident in the environment that arouses stress.

2. **Your perception of that stressor**—which determines how it affects you.

3. **Your reaction or physical and emotional response to the stressor, based on that perception**—it's not the same for everybody.

This information explains why some people view a seemingly

stressful incident calmly while other people are running in circles, panicked and screaming.

Let's take the traffic jam, for instance. One person impatiently views it as an intrusion on his freedom of movement and a maddening inconvenience, while the person in the next car may regard it as a chance to listen to a favorite CD or unwind before reentering his or her life with the family. It's the same traffic jam—but the perceptions and reactions are very different. The traffic jam is stress-*inducing* to one driver and stress-*reducing* to another driver.

> "Most people handle the vast majority of potentially stressful situations successfully."

That un-stressed driver is undoubtedly employing one of the three stress-management strategies listed below. They're the same options we all have when we feel the tension of stress building:

- Remove yourself from the situation or stressor,

- Reengineer the situation so it's no longer stressful, or

- Teach yourself to react differently regarding things you find stressful that you can't change or leave.

Prolonged, unrelieved stress is the most debilitating kind of stress, so work on taming those stressors first. Although you can list dozens of sources of stress in your life, probably very few of them are actually creating problems for you.

Most people handle the vast majority of potentially stressful situations successfully. Appropriate stress is often what provides excitement and zest in our lives, and many days would be boring if all traces of stress disappeared.

But there are those long-term stressors that can do us damage. Equally damaging is responding to a small stressor as if it were a life-threatening, fire-breathing dragon attacking you.

Here are four questions that will help you determine if a stressor deserves a five-alarm response, or can just be identified and shrugged off:

1. Is there really a legitimate threat in this situation?

2. Is your interpretation of the event more of a threat than its actuality?

3. Is the event really worth a fight?

4. If you do decide to fight, will it make any difference?

Your goal is to learn to expend an appropriate amount of energy on problems or stressors based on their long-term importance to you. If you overreact to small things (like traffic jams and lost socks), you'll use up your ability to handle stress on the small stuff. There will be no energy left to tackle the big stuff.

> "The only direction for getting off a pedestal is down."

In your volunteer ministry you will undoubtedly be challenged—that comes with the territory. At times you'll be overworked. And you'll probably feel unappreciated now and then (we all do).

But you can be attentive to your own stress, health, and happiness—and make sure that when problems arise, your presence helps resolve them, not create them.

You Aren't the Messiah

A seductive temptation for volunteer leaders is to try to be all things to all people (often referred to, appropriately enough for church volunteer ministry leaders, as the "Messiah Complex"). It leads to longer and longer hours, more and more projects, weekend and evening commitments, and eventual burnout.

It often appears easier, quicker, and more effective to do things yourself rather than invest the time and effort to recruit, train, and supervise a team for effective ministry. Besides, it's kind of nice to feel you have climbed on that pedestal called "indispensable," right? But remember: The only direction for getting off a pedestal is down, and it behooves you to climb down before you fall off.

You are *not* the Messiah! You are simply a person who works with and through others to accomplish ministry goals. And how those other people feel about working with you has . . .

tremendous impact on both the quality and quantity of work they'll do,

which has a great impact on your own perceptions of your effectiveness as a manager,

which has an awesome impact on both your own stress level and that of your subordinates,

which has a mind-boggling impact on your health and peace of mind,

which has a gargantuan impact on how many "problem volunteers" you are encountering (or creating?)—*and* how you deal with them.

If you're trying to do too much for too long, I can tell you this: When problems pop up in the ministry, one of the culprits will probably be you.

In my book, *Survival Skills for Managers*, I list several suggestions to help manage the stress in your life:

1. Clarify your value system so you're expending the greatest amount of time and energy on those things of greatest value to you.

2. Take good care of yourself physically through exercise and good nutrition.

3. Create and use personal support systems.

4. Learn to let go of past resentments, toxic relationships, and bad health habits.

5. Seek variety, and develop a well-rounded personality—avoid being a one-dimensional workaholic.

6. Maintain optimism and keep some optimists around you.

7. Try to make the workplace and work itself more enjoyable.

> 8. Don't let small things become a hassle.
> 9. Take responsibility to change what needs to be changed.
> 10. Value and develop creativity and flexibility.
> 11. Have faith that things can be different.[1]

Have I overstated my case about the importance of your personal stress management and honoring your limitations? I don't think so.

You see, most of the effective volunteer managers and leaders I've known have been, first of all, effective as *persons*. By that I mean they are well-rounded, involved, enthusiastic life-long learners who always see themselves on a "journey of becoming." As such, they're fully qualified to deal with people who are living out less than their potential, and those who are "problems" because they're stressed, in the wrong job, or have determined to handle life's problems in ways that—sadly—irritate others!

We can only approach those folks with love and kindness when we have the emotional and spiritual energy to do so. Will we seek to redeem every problem situation and its participants for the good? Yes, but we'll also approach these persons with firmness and decisiveness.

Why? Because our volunteer ministry is at stake. Kingdom work must move forward.

Could the Problem Be Unresolved Conflict?

Any time we get serious about accountability, we'll run into conflict. That can be uncomfortable for Christians because we figure that if we truly love one another—like the Bible says!—then interpersonal discord won't happen.

> "We become chronic avoiders and deniers."

The result is that we become chronic avoiders and deniers. We let conflicts fester instead of dealing with them openly and well.

One of the best resources I've seen on this subject is a video by Elaine Yarbrough titled *Managing Conflict*.[2] I'm sure that some of my thoughts about conflict resolution are hers, filtered through my experience. One of the most eye-opening discoveries I've made about conflict is that there's a positive, productive side to it—and a positive, productive way to deal with it.

Consider . . .

- When in conflict, seek a resolution that everyone involved can accept. It's not always a "win-lose" situation. With creativity and resolve we can usually find a "win-win" solution.

- Remember that conflict produces lots of energy. We get fired up and passionate. Let's remember to use that energy for good, especially directing it toward problem solving.

- As you seek resolution, be sure you're digging down to the real issues, not just the on-the-surface presenting problems. It's easy to solve the wrong problems just so we can say we solved something.

- Keep in mind that conflict is neither good nor bad. It simply is.

- Make problem-solving your goal rather than trying to make everyone happy and friendly. Not everyone may emerge happy, but they can emerge heard and valued.

> "Conflict is neither good nor bad."

The first thing for us to accept is something that probably feels completely wrong: *Conflict is not bad*. It's not good, either. Conflict simply exists. It's the by-product of having so many of us crowded onto this planet, each of us with our own agendas, interests, goals, and values. We come into conflict because we're all here. About the only place you can pack people close together without conflict erupting is in a cemetery.

What's required is that we choose to not let conflict poison our relationships. Instead, we can let it be a powerful catalyst for significant change—perhaps change for the better.

Conflict itself isn't fun or painless. But it's not always bad, either, as demonstrated by how tough times, challenges, obstacles, and even affliction can prompt our spiritual growth. Consider this passage from the book of James:

> *Consider it pure joy, my brothers, whenever you face trials of many kinds, because you know that the testing of your faith develops perseverance. Perseverance must finish its work so that you may be mature and complete, not lacking anything. (James 1:2-4)*

When you encounter conflict—and you will—keep in mind that, if we choose:

Our trials can produce patience.

Our sufferings can produce mercy.

Our sicknesses can produce antibodies.

Our loneliness can produce compassion.

Our sadness can produce pity.

Our anger can produce righteous action for change.

I'd like to suggest that when conflict arises, you choose to make your first response (after the initial shock or pain): "I wonder what new—and potentially wonderful—results this situation could produce?"

Conflict always generates great energy; your job is to direct and focus that energy toward problem-solving activity rather than toward people-destroying activity. Learning to make conflict constructive makes working with volunteers even more fun and rewarding.

It takes some effort to make conflict into something positive, of course. I think two essential skills are needed:

1. To know when you're "stuck"—and how to get unstuck with certain conflict-diffusing techniques, and

2. To master four steps to reaching agreements.

The rest of this chapter will help equip you in both areas. While having conflict is neither good nor bad, letting conflict simmer and stew is most definitely *not* good.

When You Get Stuck

When conflicts arise, you need to seek a win-win solution—one where everyone involved is heard, understood, and emerges with something he or she needs.

The following techniques can help you get "unstuck" and move toward a win-win solution. These techniques will help defuse a conflict situation. Keep in mind they're just tools and temporary fixes, though—you don't want to slap an adhesive bandage on a broken bone and assume everything will heal up fine.

When you find yourself in conflict, invest the time to resolve it thoroughly.

Use "I" statements.

When you express feelings in a conflict situation, it's wise to use "I" statements rather than "you" statements. It's easier to avoid making accusations—or appearing to make accusations—when you're talking about your own feelings rather than the other person's feelings

Confronting, even with the best of intentions and with heartfelt love and concern for the other person, is a volatile process. It's better to share what you know to be true (your feelings and motivations) rather than what you only assume to be true (the other person's feelings and motivations).

> **"Confronting is a volatile process."**

Here's an example of the difference in these approaches. You'll note that both comments refer to the same event. At the church board meeting there was a comment made about Frank. Now Frank is talking with the person who made the comment.

Using an "I" statement: *"I feel bad about something I heard in the meeting last night. I'd like to talk it over."* Notice that this sounds like a report, not an attack. Frank is owning his feelings.

Using a "you" statement: *"You said something hurtful last night. You need to deal with it."* This sounds like an accusation—an attack. The person Frank is confronting will likely grow defensive very quickly.

See the difference? Who would you rather talk with about a problem or conflict: someone using "I" statements or someone who is on the offensive?

Try turning these examples of confrontation into "I" statements:

> "You never send out the agenda far enough in advance. You're not giving me time to prepare for our meetings."

_____

_____

_____

_____

> (Here's one possible revision of the statement above: *"I've noticed that I'm receiving the agenda pretty close to our meeting times. But I'd like more time to prepare."*)

"Clearly, you don't care how I might be hurt by this."

_____

_____

_____

_____

"Some of us in this program think you're being insensitive about causing embarrassment."

_____

_____

_____

_____

> "Let go of the belief that for you to personally be successful in resolving conflict, everyone must come out liking you. . . . Keep in mind that people around you need you to be effective more than they need you to be nice."—Sue Vineyard [3]

Use a "when-feel-please" formula when confronting others.

This is an excellent way to frame your statements when you have a (usually minor) grievance about someone's behavior that you need to raise—without starting a fight. It's direct, incorporates an "I" statement, and is specific about what can be done to remedy the situation. Your comment to the person with whom you have conflict combines these three elements. Here's how the three-part statement works:

1. Identify when the issue arose: "When you open the windows early in the morning . . ."

2. Identify a feeling: "I begin to feel cold . . ."

3. Use the word *please*: "So, could you please wait until later in the day to do that?"

Here are some other examples:

"When you come home late without warning, I feel neglected and unimportant. Honey, please give me a phone call when you know you're going to be late."

"When you tell the guys at the club about an upcoming church meeting, I feel left out of the loop. Could you please call or send me an email, since I'm not a club member?"

Avoid rhetorical questions.

Need I say more here? We all do it, so see if you recognize yourself in any of these questioning statements—whether they've been uttered at home, school, work, or church:

"Why can't I depend on you?"

"Why can't you see that you're putting people off?"

"Wouldn't it be better if you just _____?"

"Why can't you be more like your brother?"

"Why do you say such things?"

"Is this casserole too salty or what?"

"Why can't you ever learn?"

"Who said you could do that?"

Most rhetorical attacks start with the question "Why," which is usually a clue that what follows will be worthless for increasing understanding and cooperation. "Why" is one of the least effective approaches to resolving conflict; questioning is a great way to fan flames of anger.

Instead, state your feelings, needs, and ideas directly.

Leave all sarcasm behind—forever.

Humor in relationships is dangerous. A well-placed joke can work wonders in a tense situation, but joking can also backfire. It's often not worth the risk to make light of something that's potentially a sore subject between you and another person.

> "Here's Marlene's Rule about Sarcasm: Banish it."

My advice is that you should avoid joking with volunteers. If you do choose to joke with a volunteer, be wise. Know who you're dealing with. Be sure what you're saying cannot be construed as offensive—and that's tough to do!

And here's Marlene's Rule about Sarcasm: Banish it. It's *never* worth the risk. It offers a multitude of opportunities for misinterpretation and hurt feelings. What you say may sound cute at the time, but it will come back to haunt you later.

Four Steps for Getting to an Agreement

There's no right or wrong way to reach agreements when people are in conflict. Whatever works . . . works! However, I'd like to summarize four basic steps that often produce an excellent chance of reaching good agreements.

Step 1: Discover and emphasize what the participants hold in common.

You discover common ground by bringing people together and getting them sharing about "where they are." Ask everyone to respectfully take a turn speaking, and ask that everyone else respectfully listen without comment.

Your job is to note the areas, no matter how small, where people already agree. These are the places to begin building an even broader "island" of agreement. After sharing, highlight areas of agreement. Everyone may be surprised at the common ground already held!

Step 2: Attempt to "un-freeze" stalemates.

During the sharing you'll uncover specific places where conflicting parties are in an apparent deadlock. For instance, some volunteers want your instructional program to be held during morning hours. They are quite adamant about this because it fits with their home and school schedules.

Other participants demand an evening program that won't cut into their day jobs. In order to work at bringing the sides to some kind of resolution, you might try one or more of these approaches:

- **String it out.** Not every conflict can be solved in one sitting. Your first goal may be to get agreement that you'll meet several times to deal with the conflict.

- **Reduce the personal pain.** Explore what it is about a solution that causes the most pain for persons on either side of the issue. How can you eliminate or reduce some of that pain? For example, could you arrange for morning childcare for those who need to be home until noon?

- **Suggest pay-offs.** What will it take to get people to accept a less than ideal solution? Can you compensate or reward them in ways that make it worthwhile for them to re-arrange their work schedules?

• **Create compromises.** Get both sides to agree to give in so that they can meet in the middle. For example, meet in the evening during the first month, and in the morning during the second month.

• **Find a new alternative.** One side wants a morning program, and the other side wants an evening program. But what if instead of meeting as a group for instruction, you set up a system of one-on-one mentoring? Then pairs of individuals could meet together based on their own personal schedules.

The key: Creatively brainstorm solutions without setting limits. In the initial stages everyone should know that no possible solution will be considered foolish or out of bounds. Let the possibilities be raised and "placed in the hopper" for future consideration. Creative thinking is the key.

> "Creatively brainstorm solutions without setting limits."

Step 3: Produce a written contract that outlines all specific agreements between the parties.

Make this summary as clear and as simple as possible. This can be as simple as e-mailing meeting minutes with a clear statement about how the conflict was resolved and how people agreed to proceed. Or it can be a more formal document that's filed in the church office, perhaps after everyone has signed it. Use your common sense about how elaborate you need to be, based on the gravity of the issues.

Don't generalize; be specific. And consider building in consequences everyone is aware of, should one or more persons break the agreement.

Step 4: Schedule a follow-up meeting.

This meeting creates an opportunity for your evaluation process, and guarantees that you won't come to agreements and then forget about them. It's human nature to slip back into old patterns of conflict unless we're diligent about monitoring our progress.

1. Marlene Wilson, *Survival Skills for Managers* (Boulder, Colo.: Volunteer Management Associates, 1981), pp. 189-221.

2. The video *Managing Conflict* (1997) by Elaine Yarbrough is from the Yarbrough Group, 1113 Spruce Street, Boulder, Colorado 80302. Phone: (303) 449-7107.

3. Sue Vineyard, *Stop Managing Volunteers* (Downers Grove, Ill.: Heritage Arts Publishing, 1996), p. 88.

FOUR
Accountability: Evaluating Volunteers

Discover how to make evaluations friendly, not frightening. Doing evaluations in a way that's helpful. Plus, how to handle difficult volunteers.

Uh oh . . . a problem has arisen. You look at the system for solutions. You look to your own stress levels and check for burnout. Then you work toward constructive conflict resolution if there's a disagreement.

But suppose the root of the problem turns out to be a particular volunteer? And no matter how much you try to find a solution, every finger keeps pointing back to that one specific person?

"Problem volunteers" are rare but they do happen. When it comes to evaluating a volunteer who's a problem, let me urge you to embrace these two accountability principles that need to be applied to *all* volunteers:

1. Never lower standards for volunteers. It's the ultimate put-down for volunteers to feel that what they do is so unimportant that it doesn't matter if they do it well—or even at all.

2. View volunteers as unpaid staff and always hold them accountable for their commitments and actions. If it would matter if your paid pastor did it, it matters if a volunteer does it—or doesn't do it. Treat paid and unpaid staff the same.

> "Problem volunteers" are rare but they do happen."

What Exactly Is a "Problem Volunteer"?

If a volunteer is unable to function in his or her role, that's a problem . . . but he or she may *not* be a problem volunteer.

If you see that the problems generated by a volunteer far outweigh the good coming from his or her efforts, or if that volunteer is intentionally making things difficult for everyone and therefore damaging your team or volunteer ministry, *that's* a problem volunteer.

So how do you handle that sort of person?

Let's approach this issue in two ways: by being *proactive* and *reactive*.

We'll focus on proactively preventing problem-volunteer situations in the first place—by making sure we're conducting ongoing performance reviews. Being proactive is one way you can make certain you very seldom, if ever, see a problem volunteer.

Then we'll talk about being reactive—how to react when it's obvious that no solution other than separating a volunteer from your program will work to keep your ministry healthy.

Being Proactive

The great news is that you can prevent lots of problems in your volunteer ministry simply by being proactive with evaluations (also called performance reviews). After all, performance reviews have the potential to be overwhelmingly positive—and most are!

> "Think of performance evaluations as an *affirming* event."

I want to encourage you to think of performance evaluations as an *affirming* event, not one to be feared, ignored, or (as in some church settings) avoided. They're times we can celebrate what volunteers have accomplished and what a difference they're making in the church.

If you're focusing on the "well-dones" as well as the areas that could use improvement, you'll find your conversation well-seasoned with words like *success, growth, affirm, new opportunity,* and *mentor.* When volunteers walk away from their evaluations, they should feel ten feet high, even if you've identified some things to work on.

Why?

Because volunteers *want* to get better at what they do. They *appreciate* your taking the time to carefully observe them and suggest ways they can make an even bigger impact. Volunteers are *grateful* you notice and take them seriously.

See why evaluations can be a fun time?

Betty Stallings helps us look at the review process in a nutshell, using four key concepts:[1]

Key Concept 1: Schedule reviews with regularity.

Successful performance reviews connect the person who assigns the work with the person who does it, so the two can talk. It may seem obvious that this is a good idea, but it's amazing how many churches fail to schedule such periodic reviews, although the church can only benefit from such a move (see concept 2).

In the review meetings, volunteer and leader discuss what they expect from themselves and each other and how well those expectations are being met. Performance reviews should be nonthreatening, constructive, supportive, flexible, and empowering. The aim: to encourage volunteers to stretch for high standards and determine how the church can help the volunteer achieve his or her goals.

Performance reviews can be effective and renewing. But that won't happen automatically. Here are the essential elements for success:

1. As they enter the organization, volunteers should be told of the feedback system, including the system of performance reviews.

2. Be sure both the volunteer and supervisor share how things are going.

3. Base performance reviews on previously agreed-upon standards, job descriptions, tasks, deadlines, available resources, and intervening circumstances.

4. Avoid surprises. If ongoing supervision and conflict resolution have taken place there will be no new issues raised at the review.

5. Depending on the size and culture of your church, the process can be formal or informal. Do what makes sense.

6. It's best to gradually include current volunteers who have not previously been reviewed. Self-assessment may work best as the system is initiated.

7. Schedule reviews for a specific time or they'll be put off.

Key Concept 2: Benefit from the reviews.

You'll discover all kinds of benefits—to the volunteers and to your entire organization—when you start using volunteer performance reviews. Here's a short list of benefits:

1. The process is a strong statement that volunteers are important and that both volunteers and organizations are held accountable to their agreements.

2. Reviews are encouraging, since volunteers want to be successful and typically respond well to feedback.

3. Reviews are a good time to express appreciation for volunteer efforts and acknowledge accomplishments.

4. Reviews enable volunteers and volunteer ministries to re-negotiate their working agreement for the next time period.

5. Reviews provide an opportunity for planning to improve volunteer performance in the future (for example, training or new placement).

6. Reviews allow volunteers to express concerns and "escape" an unfavorable situation.

7. Reviews allow staff to share concerns and "dismiss" a volunteer if the situation requires that action.

Key Concept 3: Define it, with agreed-upon standards.

At the heart of a good volunteer review is a clear description of volunteer job responsibilities and success indicators. Plus, you and your volunteer should have a shared view of

Barriers to Effective Performance Reviews

Betty Stallings often asks her workshop participants: "What are potential barriers your organization will need to overcome to do performance reviews successfully?" Here are some of the typical responses and strategies for overcoming the barriers:

"Even our staff isn't reviewed."
Initiate reviews with staff before initiating volunteer reviews.

"We don't have any policies on reviewing volunteers."
Work together to institute policies on performance reviews and dismissal.

"Current volunteers are resisting the idea."
Involve current volunteers in developing the forms and processes.

Here's an outline for a performance-review process that incorporates concept 3.

Before the Session

1. Have the volunteer fill out a self-assessment form.

2. Review the volunteer's job description, goals, and standards, and evaluate "job performance" (how volunteers did their jobs) versus "job expectation" (how volunteers were expected to do their jobs).

3. Do a performance review based on the job expectation versus job performance.

During the Session

1. Together, review the agreed-upon job expectations.

2. Share positive feedback and give appreciation for service.

3. Volunteer: share self-assessment and assessment of church support.

4. Supervisor: share assessment of volunteer's performance.

5. Discuss any barriers that volunteer experienced in carrying out the position.

6. Discuss future plans for the volunteer in the organization (such as position or goals).

After the Session

1. Write a report for the volunteer's file.

2. Follow-up on action plans or agreements made.

hoped-for outcomes and agree on what factors will contribute to those outcomes.

Key Concept 4: Decide it, and take action.

Outcomes from volunteer performance reviews can range from "applause" to dismissal—by the supervisor or by the volunteer.

One way to keep volunteers continually involved in your ministry is to use reviews as a time to discuss a volunteer's readiness for a new challenge, the need for a change, or the desire to take a break for awhile. These are all legitimate reasons that a volunteer may leave your ministry, at least temporarily.

> "Use reviews as a time to discuss a volunteer's readiness for a new challenge."

As a side note, when your reviews frequently point to significant problems meeting expectations, you might look into productivity and morale. If there's been low productivity or morale on the part of the volunteer, it's important to discuss remedies. Here are some of the possible reasons you'll want to explore:

- Is the volunteer bored with the routine?

- Are there personality differences between the volunteer and his or her supervisor, or on the team?

- Is there idleness because of a fluctuating workload or insufficient staff?

- Is there a lack of interest in the work?

- Are the assignments poorly defined?

- Is there inadequate supervision and/or training?

- Are policies misunderstood?

- Is there resentment because of too much work or unrealistic deadlines?

- Is there poor communication within the work team (staff/volunteers)?

- Is the volunteer experiencing emotional stress and personal difficulties?

- Is participation erratic?

- Does the volunteer feel appreciated?

- Have staff or organizational changes impacted the volunteer?

- Is there staff resistance to utilizing volunteers?

The flip side of evaluating a volunteer's performance is to first know whether you're meeting *their* legitimate, ongoing needs. Something I ask potential volunteers who have a history of volunteerism is why they left the last place they volunteered.

I've been astounded at how frequently I heard things such as:

"I never knew what they wanted me to do."

"I didn't even have a job description."

"I didn't know who I was responsible to, so I never knew who to go to with questions, ideas, or problems."

"They never provided any training to help me do what I was asked to do."

"Nobody ever told me if what I was doing was helpful or not."

"I was asked to do more and more, and I finally just burned out!"

Here's what volunteers repeatedly have said they want and need:

- To be carefully interviewed and appropriately assigned to a meaningful task

- To receive training and supervision to enable them to do that task well

- To be involved in planning and evaluating the program in which they participate

- To receive recognition in a way that is meaningful to them

- To be regarded as unique persons

- To be accepted as a valued member of the team

Are you currently providing those things to your volunteers? Don't assume you are: *Ask*. See what volunteers tell you.

To a great extent, how a volunteer performs reflects directly on the volunteer's supervisor. It's the supervisor who provides training, equipping, encouragement, and supervision.

If you provide what volunteers legitimately need, you'll hang on to your people longer, they'll be more fulfilled and effective, and you'll see better performance. All of which translates to far happier volunteers—and fewer "problem volunteers."

Advice for Those Just Starting to Do Performance Reviews

Like most things, you get better at doing reviews the more you do them. If you're new at this, perhaps this short list of suggestions will help.

Do be clear about a volunteer's interests and needs.

When you meet with a volunteer to do an evaluation, it's not about you. It's about the volunteer. So before you present a list of things you think the volunteer could do better, show a genuine concern for the volunteer's needs.

Keep in mind that back when you or a colleague first interviewed the volunteer, you gathered information about the volunteer's interests. The review is a wonderful time to explore if the volunteer's experience has matched initial expectations.

You can get at how reality is matching expectations by exploring . . .

- Does the volunteer's position connect with his or her interests?

- Is the volunteer still interested in the position?

- Does the volunteer enjoy serving in the position?

- Have relationships formed that make serving in the position fun for the volunteer?

- Is the volunteer satisfied with his or her level of involvement in planning, implementing, and evaluating in the ministry area?

Do clarify a volunteer's current interests by asking the right questions.

Here are some questions you'll find helpful to ask . . .

- What if?

- What will it take?

- Why not?

- What would be the perfect situation?

- How do you like to be treated?

- What problem(s) are we trying to solve?

- What is your goal?

- What concerns you the most?

- When are you most irritated? most satisfied?

- What's a situation when things went well?

- What do you want? What would it mean if you got it?

Do be professional about the review process.

Do performance reviews one-on-one and respect confidentiality. Make the process feel safe for volunteers. You can hold a review in a coffee shop, on the subway, or sitting on a park bench as long as you're both comfortable and feel confident you won't be overheard. The location of the discussion isn't what makes it "professional." Your attitude does that.

Do provide an opportunity for volunteers to evaluate their own performance.

When you ask, "How do you think you did?" you learn a *lot*. And while volunteers are speaking, listen attentively so you can ask follow-up questions.

Do be positive and focus on achievements at least as much as the areas that need improvement.

Again—make evaluations positive experiences.

Do make the discussion a dialogue, not a monologue.

If you're doing all the talking, you're missing much of the benefit of the review process. Be sure you ask questions and then give volunteers the encouragement and time to answer. Expect give and take, and be prepared to answer questions as well as ask them.

Do bring the job description and any other written materials related to the volunteer's position.

You'll want to review them and may, if the situation calls for it, make changes. Keep the option open for making changes to accommodate the volunteer and strengthen the volunteer ministry.

Do summarize what was discussed and decided.

It's helpful for you to get together briefly later so both you and the volunteer can sign the summary. As you read through it and make sure it's accurate, you have yet another chance to clarify the information.

Do be open to change.

Things change. People change. Goals change. Use the performance review to check out whether the volunteer wants to change directions or the terms of his or her service. Maybe with a new baby in the house it's time to take off six months or a year. Perhaps the fact the volunteer recently retired means she's open to taking on more responsibility. Not all change is bad!

And here's something you *don't* want to do . . .

Don't neglect your mentoring responsibility.

Mentoring and coaching can be the most rewarding parts of your job. Catch your volunteers doing good things and applaud them. If you see something positive, reinforce the behavior and celebrate it together.

The flip side of this is to watch for the other kinds of routine activities they may be doing—things that are just making everything harder for them.

I once watched a brand new carpenter's apprentice trying to nail two 2-by-4 boards together at the ends, to form a right angle. He put the boards on the ground and began nailing. But as he hit the nail, both the boards would move a foot or two away from him. He kept at it for an agonizing several minutes. Eventually, the foreman came over and, with an irritated look, said: "Watch." The experienced carpenter stepped on the ends of both pieces and quickly pounded in the nails.

Are there times like that in the volunteer program? You'd better believe it. Keep your eyes wide open, and you'll see people doing all sorts of unproductive things because they're inexperienced.

> "If you see something positive, reinforce the behavior."

They need someone to gently suggest a better approach. That's the way good coaches and mentors do it. And when important learning takes place, a warm feeling of "mission accomplished" begins to spread throughout the ministry.

Being Reactive

I once had a troublesome volunteer working for me when I was executive director of a volunteer agency. Jill (not her real name) was creating a problem for other volunteers and, as the director, it was my place to deal with the situation.

I became aware of the problem when three different volunteers separately told me they didn't want to work in the Volunteer Center on Tuesdays. When I inquired what was happening on Tuesdays, they reluctantly told me they didn't like working with Jill. They said she was extremely bossy and always telling them what to do, though she wasn't a supervisor.

Note that the problem was already in place. Jill was one of those rare "problem volunteers" that I said appear very infrequently. But there she was . . . and she was creating a problem that was costing me volunteers.

Let me tell you how I handled it so you can benefit from my experience.

The first thing I did was check out the information personally rather than take someone else's word for it. In this case, I stayed in the office the next Tuesday and saw that Jill was indeed bossing everyone around. What the volunteers had reported to me was accurate.

It's my policy—and I'd suggest it be yours—to never confront in public. I asked Jill to stay after work so we could talk privately. She agreed, and once the rest of the staff left, the two of us sat down in comfortable chairs.

> "As the director, it was my place to deal with the situation."

I stated honestly what the problem was, being as specific as possible in describing the behavior I'd seen with my own eyes. I asked Jill if she was aware of the effect her behavior was having on the other volunteers. Jill said she wasn't aware of any impact, so I told her that three volunteers had asked not to work with her because she bossed them around. Jill shrugged and said, "Oh, I've always been like that."

Jill's response wasn't unexpected. The world is full of people who aren't aware of the speed with which they roar through life or the volume at which they operate. In Jill's case, she simply didn't see any problem in having a take-charge attitude that had probably served her well other places in her life.

Except that attitude wasn't helping in the Center. I told Jill I wanted us to come up with a mutually agreeable solution to the problem. I explained to Jill that her behavior wasn't acceptable and that we needed to arrive at some solution before she left.

I invited Jill to offer her suggestions first, and she just sat there, staring at the floor, the wall, at anything but me. So I then suggested the solutions I had jotted down beforehand as I considered how to resolve the solution—without losing Jill.

It's important for you to understand that the goal of our talk wasn't to rewire Jill so she was meek and mild. That wasn't going to happen, and I certainly didn't have any right to demand it.

And I didn't necessarily want to lose Jill as a volunteer. I was willing to do so, but that was by no means my first choice! I wanted her to understand that.

So I suggested Jill could work alone in the back office, or perhaps she could consider volunteering somewhere else. She rejected both these options because she was lonely, and we at the Center were her "family."

Finally, Jill reluctantly said, "Well, I guess I could stop doing it."

I enthusiastically supported that suggestion!

"But," I said, "you told me you've been bossy all your life, so this is going to be a hard behavior to change." I insisted that we set a date to meet once a week to chat for a few minutes about how she was progressing. I also told her I would be getting feedback from her fellow volunteers to hear about how she was doing.

I followed up. We met weekly for over two months. The first few weeks the reports were that "Jill was genuinely trying," and eventually I heard, "She's improving!" Finally the volunteers were reporting that they found they really liked Jill, and enjoyed working with her.

> "Never confront in public."

The day came when Jill and I met for our weekly meeting and I said, "Congratulations! Behavior change isn't easy, but you did it. We don't need to meet any more."

Jill stood up and said to me, "This wasn't easy for you, was it? You must have cared about me quite a bit."

I replied that no, it wasn't easy, but I *did* care for her a great deal. She added, "People have disliked me all my life, and nobody ever bothered to tell me why. Thank you."

This was a significant growth experience for us both. I'm also happy to say that Jill stayed on as a volunteer at the Center for five more years.

In all my decades of experience in volunteer management, I've had to encourage just one volunteer to leave—and that was because of a breach in confidentiality. I truly believe that as you put into practice the sound principles we're encouraging in this series, such situations will be extremely rare.

Nevertheless, we do have to face the possibility: Suppose a volunteer goofs up consistently and over the long-haul? Can we ever "fire" them? I hear this question in every volunteer leadership training session I lead.

My basic response is that if you're serious about holding volunteers accountable and they fail to do the job, or they have inappropriate attitudes, boss others around, or procrastinate repeatedly, then you must react accordingly. Ask yourself, "What would I do if I were paying this person to do this job?" . . . and then do it!

First, review the job description with the individual to see if he or she is clear about what originally was agreed upon. It's amazing how often this first step clears up the problem.

Second, clarify the problem and be explicit about your expectations.

Third, examine the alternatives together. What would it take to fix the problem? Is it a change of behavior or attitude, meeting deadlines, changing ministry jobs, fixing the system, or providing training? What are the options?

"This was a significant growth experience for us both."

Finally, agree on an alternative, and set a time line to implement it. Monitor the progress, giving support and affirmation along the way.

If the volunteer either doesn't follow through—even after two to three chances—or is nasty about being held accountable, I'd "fire" the person. If you keep rescuing the individual, you both lose. This is a hard truth, but tough love may be your only option.

Here are seven guiding principles to keep in mind if you decide to let someone go . . .

- **Use direct dialogue.** You have a tough task when termination becomes necessary. It won't get any easier if you avoid the hard truths, or try to candy-coat the problems this person is creating. Meet the issues head on, and avoid talking with third parties—even if the volunteer has already done this.

- **Document the process.** There's a great deal of emotion in play; use a process and documentation (a sample termination form is provided below) to help you stay on track. You need to be able to clearly state the events and actions that brought you to the place of asking someone to leave the volunteer ministry.

> "What would it take to fix the problem?"

- **Handle the dismissal privately.** Jesus put it like this in Matthew 18:15: "If your brother sins against you, go and show him his fault, just between the two of you. If he listens to you, you have won your brother over."

- **Search together for a better fit.** Maybe this particular person just needs to find the right place. For example, if this person is having trouble getting along with others, there may be a volunteer position she can handle without lots of daily interpersonal interactions. Can this person do a great job of creating a web site, organizing e-mails, writing the bulletin each week, or overseeing computer maintenance? Be creative in this exploration together! The so-called "problem volunteer" may become an ideal kingdom worker once his or her true abilities, skills, and passions are uncovered and put to use in the church.

- **Keep your focus on the program goals.** The conflict-solving process, even if it involves termination, isn't the end of the story. Getting the volunteer ministry back on track and the terminated volunteer placed elsewhere in God-glorifying, kingdom-building, fulfilling service are what you want. This conflict shouldn't be a permanent barrier to Christian unity.

- **Agree on a follow-up schedule.** You're not trying to remove this person from the church! But when volunteers feel hurt or believe an injustice has been done, they'll sometimes cut themselves off from fellowship.

Sample Termination Interview

Volunteer Name: _____

Date of Interview:_____

Summary of reasons for termination:
(*Document the events, problems, and tasks.*)

Interview Checklist:
Be sure you cover each of these items:

___ Discuss and complete this evaluation.

___ Explore alternative jobs.
   If jobs were proposed, list what they were and
   whether they were accepted or rejected.

___ Agree on specific follow-up plans.

___ Schedule follow-up meeting.

   Date of meeting: _____ Location: _____

___ Extend continued church fellowship.

___ Pray together.
   Mutually recognize God's leading and grace in
   this matter.

___ Other:

To Be Used at Follow-up Meeting:

___ Determine if the individual is active in ministry. If so, where? Is the new ministry role satisfactory to the volunteer? Why or why not?

___ Determine if the individual is involved in the fellowship of the church. Why or why not?

Be available for spiritual counsel and mentoring, and communicate clearly that the transaction wasn't personal but instead a systemic and organizational necessity.

> "Conflict shouldn't be a permanent barrier to Christian unity."

- **Notify others who will be affected.** You'll need to tell certain members, staff, and others that the volunteer will no longer be with the ministry. Do this in an objective manner and make sure your notification method leaves no subtle insinuations or innuendoes. Be sure you communicate *exactly* what you want to say. In most cases, you won't have to explain reasons or causes.

Finally, at the risk of overstating my case, I want to emphasize how rare it will be that anyone will ever be asked to leave your ministry. In fact, if you're putting into practice the principles outlined in this series, *you will never have to face that unpleasant task.* You see, the authors of this series firmly believe that volunteer motivation and retention are the result of doing other things right—most of which you're probably already doing in an excellent way.

Among these practices are . . .

- Valuing relationships and celebrating them.

- Valuing experiential, applicable, and learner-centered training for volunteers.

- Respecting volunteers as full partners in ministry.

- Monitoring volunteers for signs of burnout.

- Conducting regular performance reviews.

- Fostering an environment where there's no put-down humor or victims.

- Creating a culture that volunteers can count on to be fair, forgiving, and fun.

Read that last word again . . . *fun!*

I use the word generously when I talk about working with volunteers because it's really the story of my life with them. I can't imagine how it could be different for you. After all, I figure you're already doing many of these things listed above—and many other good things too. If so, then I know you're enjoying working with your volunteers. Just keep loving them and treasuring their fellowship.

1. The information in the "Key Concepts" section draws heavily upon Betty Stalling's workshop on "Evaluation," pp. I-6 thru I-12.

FIVE
Encouragement through Recognition

You're already encouraging volunteers through interviews, careful placement, and positive evaluations. Now add recognition to the mix and delight your volunteers even more!

Betty Stallings is a recognition expert. One thing she emphasizes is that we tend to think of recognition as the last thing we do for a volunteer after they've finished a project, and just before he or she heads off into the sunset.

Not true! In this chapter I'm going to let Betty describe how recognition—and the encouragement it provides—can be infused throughout your ministries . . . and throughout a volunteer's experience.[1]

Betty herself caught the "disease of volunteering," as she puts it, from her father. Here is her story—and her valuable insights about recognition in volunteer ministry.

A Treasure

At the time, Betty's father was 86 years old and had lived in a multi-care institution for nearly five years. The one thing that made him feel important was serving on different committees.

About a year earlier he'd gone to visit Betty in California, intending to stay for a week. He got off the plane in his wheelchair, a little bag tucked onto his lap. When Betty and her father reached her house, he went right to his room to unpack, then called Betty in to see what he'd carried so carefully in the little bag on his lap.

He pulled out an undershirt and carefully unfolded it. Nestled inside was a coffee cup bearing this inscription: "You are a treasure."

"Daddy, who else knows this about you?" Betty asked.

He sat up straight and said, "I'm the treasurer of the Recycling Club at the home."

Betty's first thought was that letting her dad be the treasurer of *anything* was a frightening thought.

"But then I stopped to feel gratitude," Betty says. "Some caring person had taken time to see my 86-year-old father and notice that he was, indeed, a treasure. And my father cherished the gesture enough to carry a coffee cup from Boston to California to show his daughter."

> "Daddy, who else knows this about you?"

That kind of encouragement and recognition is what keeps us alive. We make an incredible impact when we remind each other what treasures we are in each others' lives, even with something as simple as a coffee cup. Those little reminders keep us going through the tough times, because we know we're not alone. Somebody noticed.

Recognizing and encouraging volunteers is a huge part of your calling as the leader of a volunteer ministry. So let's dive into how you can be effective.

We'll start by thinking about a time you were—or weren't—recognized in a volunteer role.

Then we'll explore what Betty calls the "Four P's of Recognition"—making it Personal, Plentiful, Powerful, and Practical.

Next, we'll find that not all people like to be recognized in the same way, and you'll discover techniques for delivering the perfect touch at just the right time to keep your volunteers encouraged and recognized.

Finally, we'll wrap up with a list of recognition ideas you can use right away in your own volunteer ministry.

How Have You Been Recognized?

Think about your own recognition experiences . . .

Describe a volunteer job you've held at some time in your life. Why did you hold that job?

What motivated you to do—and keep doing—this job?

In what ways did that organization recognize you? What was meaningful, and what wasn't meaningful?

What did this experience teach you about recognition of volunteers?

What is your current philosophy about recognition? What shaped it?

For your recognition efforts to be encouraging to your volunteers rather than a nuisance, I'd suggest your efforts include four characteristics:

Recognition Must Be PERSONAL

One person who filled in a chart like the one shown here concluded: "Recognition is a very personal thing. You have to know the persons you're recognizing. If you don't know them, it can be a really horrible experience. But if you know them and recognize them, it'll be an experience that will be with them forever."

Personalizing recognition efforts means you'll never again find yourself sitting through a discussion like this one:

"So, how are we going to recognize volunteers this year?"

"Let's give them plaques. I think plaques are great! People love plaques."

"Plaques? I *hate* plaques! Why don't we give them a flower pot to put on their desks?"

"That's hokey! Who wants flowers? They just die and you have to throw them away."

Notice that every comment about what might be a great recognition reflects a personal bias about what the speaker enjoys or doesn't enjoy. It's not about the volunteers at all.

The best recognition offers personal validation. You place a person in the right job. Then you notice what this particular individual wants and needs, and you fulfill those wants and needs. That's 95 percent of recognition.

If we've put people in the wrong jobs, then our creative recognition ideas won't help much. And if we don't understand what's motivating a volunteer, we can't recognize the volunteer appropriately.

But if we know the person and what motivates him or her, we can zero in on a recognition that will be meaningful. Following are four suggestions Betty shares about how to narrow down your thinking until you've got the perfect idea.

1. Make it special for just little ol' her. An organization for which I worked sent me a card on October 13th. It wasn't a national holiday but it *was* my anniversary as a staff member. That date was special only to me; someone had kept track of my time at that company and noticed the passing of exactly one year. I felt truly and deeply honored, though I can't remember a single word written on that card.

2. Make it a visual feast of the feat. I once helped out behind the scenes with a local theater organization. I was in the background the whole time, while the actors did their thing in the spotlight. In recognition of my service, however, the cast put a picture of the production on a plaque and wrote on it: "Betty, Thank you for helping make this play possible!" That plaque reminds me about the feats we accomplished as a team.

> "If we know the person, . . . we can zero in on a recognition that will be meaningful."

3. Make it fit the personality profile. The real challenge is to make everyone in the group feel special. But people are so different in what communicates encouragement and appreciation. How do you make sure you connect with everyone?

Although it's possible to put together an event that contains enough diverse elements to speak to each volunteer, it only works if ahead of time you ask, "How can everyone feel special when they leave this event?"

4. Make it timely—ASAP. The timeliness of recognition is important. The closer to the accomplishment or project, the better. That's why it's not necessarily the best way to wait until the end of the year or the close of the event to recognize people.

And here's a bonus idea: To recognize someone who showed up just once—invite the person back! If it was a good one-day experience, chances are the volunteer might come back again, and you've gained a new, highly motivated volunteer.

The bottom line: Recognition doesn't take that much time, but it *does* take planning, sincerity, and action on a very personal level.

Recognition Must Be PLENTIFUL

Like the old story about voting in Chicago: Do recognition early and do it often. For recognition to be encouraging, it needs to be an ongoing aspect of our overall leadership style.

Betty works with a City Council that always starts meetings with recognition of a volunteer who's doing good work in the community. They begin by patting somebody (really, themselves!) on the back for making good progress. Then they proceed on an upbeat note to tackle the problems waiting for them.

Encouraging recognition has to permeate your volunteer ministry and hopefully your church. Everyone on staff needs to be convinced of its importance, not just you. You can't be the only person recognizing others, the designated cheerleader. That won't feel right.

This means that spontaneity is just fine. Recognition will often be informal and spontaneous. And it will be more powerful for that spontaneity.

When to Recognize Volunteers

Effective recognition doesn't only happen when a project is completed. It needs to be plentiful and ongoing. Here are some quick ideas about when you can recognize people:.

- At the sign-up table

- On the first day

- Daily

- Monthly

- Annually

- At the end of a project

- On special days

- On sick days

- Upon departure

- Your ideas? Jot them below:

Recognition Must Be POWERFUL

Betty serves on a board that, at every meeting, recognizes one of its members for something they've done since the previous meeting. Sometimes it's funny, it's always spontaneous, and it's definitely effective.

Says Betty, "We all show up in case we're going to get this recognition. We know we need to be there, and because it's done at the beginning of the meeting, we know we need to arrive on time. A room full of very busy people who manage to make every meeting and on time—that's the power of even *potential* recognition!"

How Do You Say "Thanks"?

Just saying "Thank you" is powerful in itself. Here's a guide to helping you clarify what you think and feel about saying thanks.

To me, saying "Thank you" means the most when . . .

Saying "Thank you" means little if . . .

The most creative way anyone has ever thanked me was to . . .

The way we usually say "Thanks" around here is . . .

Some of the people I/we need to say "Thank You" to this week are . . .

Some creative ways to do this might be . . . (just brainstorm a little).

What did you learn about yourself here? Discuss your ideas with other leaders. What suggestions do they have?

Betty attended an event years ago in which she helped the organizer. After the event the organizer was thanking Betty for helping. As they spoke, the organizer absent-mindedly put her hand into her jacket pocket. She didn't realize there was anything in it, and Betty could tell that she was somewhat surprised to find a partial roll of Lifesavers. She smiled and handed the roll to Betty, saying, "You've been a real Lifesaver today!"

Later, speaking at a conference, I told this Lifesaver story and went on with my workshop. At the end of the day, when I returned to my desk, there on top of my papers sat a red Lifesaver. I don't know who put it there, but it was a special moment for me.

It was so small, but it was so very powerful.

Recognition Must Be PRACTICAL

You may hear objections to the practice of recognizing volunteers, which can keep you from having a truly encouraging ministry. Here's Betty's advice for addressing those excuses—most of which fall into the "it's not practical for us" category.

"There's no money in the budget for this sort of thing." Recognition doesn't have to cost a lot of money. Explain that you don't need a catered banquet—just some rolls of Lifesavers!

"Volunteers say they don't want or need recognition." Except—they do. Maybe they're saying they don't need another plaque, but be assured: They'll welcome appropriate recognition.

"The paid staff aren't even recognized!" In a church where paid staff are not recognized, there may not be enthusiasm for recognizing volunteers. Give it a try anyway. Even better: Recognize the paid staff, too! One woman told me that in her organization, the volunteers nominate staff people for recognition. I thought that was powerful and effective.

"One of our sacred cows is standing in the way of personal recognition." Nobody *says* this, of course, but it's the problem. And you can't shoot a sacred cow unless you're prepared for lots of beef(s).

Maybe someone thinks it's undignified. Or that it diminishes the value of service if someone says "thanks." Or maybe it's as simple as the fact the church has never before recognized volunteers, and therefore it isn't something that needs to be done now. With tact and wisdom see if you can at least herd the sacred cow to one side of the aisle so you can slip past it.

> "You can't shoot a sacred cow unless you're prepared for lots of beef(s)."

When recognition is personal, plentiful, powerful, and practical, it encourages and edifies your volunteers. That's probably no surprise. What might be surprising, though, is how many people give of themselves as volunteers when they receive little or no encouragement or recognition at all.

Consider this story from Betty's life as a trainer and consultant . . .

> In one of my training sessions an elderly woman told her story of being her church's "coffee lady." She said she served coffee between services for 13 years without fail.
>
> "What did they do to recognize you over the years?" I asked.
>
> Her response was heartbreaking: "One gentleman did come up to me once at the break and said, 'Your coffee is always too cold.'"

The man at least noticed this woman's ministry. And his criticism was apparently the only form of recognition that came to a faithful servant for more than a decade.

How sad. May it never happen this way at your church. But wait . . . is it happening that way right now?

Recognizing Teams As Well As Individuals

It's great to recognize individual volunteers. But don't forget that most of our volunteer efforts are, at heart, team efforts. So it's smart to find ways to regularly celebrate, affirm, and recognize the volunteer ministry team as a whole.

A common approach is to plan an annual banquet at the end of each church year. You could make it like an "awards banquet" for a sports team, or you could make it part of a larger service of worship and praise to God.

In any case, when it comes time to recognize and affirm team members, be sure you've developed categories of excellence. Provide recognition for various achievements and outstanding work (make these honors real and deserved). If it's a celebration strictly for the leadership team, then invite all team members and celebrate the completion of one or more particular projects. Highlight every aspect of the success, and recognize the contributions of each person involved.

If your leadership group is small and you want to be less formal, then simply plan a dinner (or breakfast) out together. Make plans to highlight and celebrate team successes. You might also hand out mementos or small gifts, such as logo coffee mugs or gift certificates to appropriate stores.

Here are a few other ideas from Betty for encouraging and recognizing a team . . .

Start a Team Project scrapbook. Include memorabilia and photographs from special projects, events, and achievements.

Create a Recognition Sheet. Make it available for people to complete at any time. Leave space for the team member's name, the date, and a brief explanation of how that team member had a special impact on the ministry's success. Ask the person completing the sheet to sign it, and send it to the team leader. The team leader can then trumpet the accomplishments publicly.

Create an Affirmation Board. The same concept as above, but post the sheets of paper where everyone can see them. Ground rule: All comments must be positive and affirming!

Hand out a Team Rose. Start each leadership meeting with a time when members can recognize and affirm one another. Then together decide who will receive the single rose-in-a-vase for that week.

Schedule a team meeting as a "Surprise Celebration." You've heard of a surprise birthday party? How about a surprise

Affirmation Party? Fill the meeting room with balloons, and make refreshments available. Then celebrate all the good that's been accomplished in the past month, quarter, or year. Be specific about what has happened, and who did what. Consider blending in a time of praise and worship to the Lord, who guided and strengthened everyone involved.

Hold a staff appreciation luncheon. Use the time to say thanks and to recognize the volunteers' efforts. Don't conduct business.

Connect Recognition to Motivational Preference

I mentioned in volume 4 of this series that I have learned to recognize several kinds of people when it comes to motivational preference: Affiliators, Power People, and Achievers. I promised to suggest ways that you could provide encouragement and recognition that was tailor-made for each of these motivational preferences. I'm going to defer to the expertise of Betty Stallings once again, and share what she's learned about providing recognition for motivational preference.

Recognition Based on Motivational Type

Affiliators

   Awards and Acknowledgements
   1. Name and photo appearing in newsletter
   2. Recognition in presence of family, peers
   3. Personal notes and verbal greetings from supervisor
   4. Cards for special anniversary or birthday
   5. Gifts and notes from clients
   6. Banquets, potlucks, picnics
   7. Attending a social event with other people

   Job Benefits That Encourage Ongoing Commitment
   1. Opportunities for socialization and meeting new friends
   2. Personalized on-the-job training

Power People

Awards and Acknowledgements

1. Public recognition (in front of peers, in media)
2. Awards named for them
3. Letters of commendation noting their influential achievements or impact
4. Notes from influential people, community leaders, and other notables commenting on their effect on humankind

Job Benefits That Encourage Ongoing Commitment

1. Assignments providing opportunities for influence, teaching, and interaction with high officials
2. Assignments with impressive titles
3. Work with a good deal of authority involved
4. Board of Directors position

Achievers

Awards and Acknowledgements

1. Plaques, badges, pins (tangible awards)
2. Letters of special commendation on their achievement(s) to boss, newspaper, or school
3. An award named in their honor
4. Nomination for local, state, national awards
5. Résumé documentation
6. Promotion to a more responsible job

Job Benefits That Encourage Ongoing Commitment

1. Entire responsibility delegated to them and latitude given to them on the way it is done
2. Opportunities to set goals, create innovative ideas
3. Work to succeed or exceed a specific goal[2]

Encouragement is like a breath of fresh air in the lives of volunteers. Most people simply don't hear much encouragement or receive much recognition in daily life. It's rare—and therefore precious.

Encouragement and recognition will help you hang onto the volunteers who are already involved, and also create the sort of culture that attracts new volunteers. You've already built a wonderful culture as you have instituted job descriptions, interviews, placement, and evaluation. Excellent, encouraging recognition practices are the icing on the cake.

> **"Encouragement is rare—and therefore precious."**

In the church, all the members are part of the body of Christ. We're all working toward the same mission. We all play a crucial role.

I truly believe there are plenty of believers out there, willing and able to help us do anything that needs doing in the church. We just need to love and care for them as Christ cares for us.

Winning Encouragement and Recognition Ideas for Your Volunteer Ministry

I urge you to develop recognition methods in three categories: ideas to use regularly to provide ongoing support, ideas you will use informally, and those you will use formally for special occasions.

Some of the ideas presented below are my own; some I've gathered from others. We offer them as a way to "prime the pump" of your own creativity. Add your own ideas and then plan to implement as many as possible in the future:

To Offer Ongoing Support

- Set up a Suggestion Box for suggestions from volunteers only.

- Give a personalized coffee mug to each volunteer.

- Implement a "Release Time" each week or month. This

would be a chance for volunteers to pursue volunteer enrichment activities, or just have some time off for rest and relaxation. One Colorado church cancels all children's programming in August to give children's ministry volunteers a month off.

- Throughout the year, pay attention to the environment in which your volunteers labor and have meetings. Make surroundings pleasant, comfortable, and stocked with all the practical items and tools they need (if possible, include some "luxuries"). What a morale booster this is!

- Set up support groups for your volunteers. When these groups meet, they can share their experiences, concerns, solutions, and ideas. They can pray for one another and develop their own creative ideas for mutual self-support.

> **"Encourage volunteers to create new ministries."**

- Encourage volunteers to create new ministries that will match their skills and desires to serve (rather than always slotting people into current ministries).

- Be sure your church pays the costs and expenses of any training seminars or workshops you recommend. Schedule such events regularly for increasing volunteer competency and self-confidence.

- Invite volunteers to form a worship committee that meets with the pastor and other worship leaders. Together, plan a creative worship service that focuses around the theme of volunteer ministry—and don't recruit at the service!

To Informally Recognize Volunteers
- Send a birthday, anniversary, or Christmas card.
- Offer impromptu verbal affirmation: What's important is who gives it and what accomplishments are mentioned.

• Involve volunteers in the long-range planning of your church.

• Invite volunteers to church staff, planning, and other significant meetings.

• Regularly send out press releases to local media outlets. Tell all about the marvelous work of your volunteers in the various programs. Name names, and be specific about what is being accomplished. (As appropriate, also include information about how particular volunteers serve in other groups in the community. We're in this together!)

> **"Constantly send out thank-you notes about a job well done."**

• Constantly send out thank-you notes about a job well done, no matter how small the job may have been. It deserves praise, for it was done for the kingdom.

• Praise your volunteers to their family and friends. (How could this hurt?)

• In the church bulletin regularly or occasionally list the persons who volunteer in your church and/or the community. Regularly do this on bulletin boards and within the church newsletter, as well.

• Give small gifts occasionally, but tie them to an affirmation. Use the following examples to come up with your own individualized ideas.

What a bright idea!
(Note stuck to a light bulb.)

No one holds a candle to you!
(Scented candle or pack of birthday candles.)

You are a LIFESAVER!
(Candy with a note.)

Thanks for raisin' the tough questions!
(Mini boxes of raisins.)

To Formally Recognize Volunteers

• Have a birthday lunch once a month to celebrate all volunteer and paid staff birthdays that occurred during that month.

• Give the volunteer a promotion to a higher-level volunteer position, a more responsible job. Make it public.

• Make notes in the personnel records, and let the volunteer know it. Include a letter from the director and others that will stay on file. Document community involvement this way, too.

• Nominate a volunteer for community recognition.

• Give a gift of appreciation. For example: a certificate of recognition, a book, or other memento appropriate to the volunteer ministry. Other ideas for gifts include: pens, paperweights, coffee mugs, photographs, videos, gift baskets, concert/sports tickets (get them donated), a laminated copy of an article about them in the newspaper. Or consider giving coupons good for one day off without an excuse or lunch with the director.

• Provide opportunities for your volunteers to speak! Perhaps have a regular column in your church newsletter for the "Volunteer Viewpoint."

• Consider having a Volunteer of the Week (or month or year). Give special privileges or "perks" to this person—such as providing a special parking slot right next to the church entrance! Place their pictures in a prominent place.

Keep in mind the volunteer's job when you're giving encouragement.

There is a tremendous difference in volunteer jobs, and few differences are as significant as this one: Does the volunteer supervise others, or not?

Every volunteer position is important. Every position has its challenges. But as a ministry leader you know what stresses can come with supervising others. And that means if you're going to support and encourage your volunteers who supervise others, you've got to *supersize* that support and encouragement!

When you're considering how to encourage a volunteer, keep in mind the environment in which the volunteer serves. Some positions have more responsibility (and perhaps more stress) associated with them than other positions might have.

Here are the three general levels of responsibility we identified earlier, and some ideas for encouraging people in each:

High Responsibility Volunteer Jobs

These people are often responsible for assigning tasks to others, and actually shape areas of ministry. They have the stress of *doing* reviews as well as receiving them, so you have much in common. Make these volunteers one of your top priorities.

Ways to encourage people in this sort of position include . . .

- *Personally invest in these volunteers.* If you have an organizational chart, it's likely these volunteers report directly to you. So it makes sense for you to be providing extra mentoring opportunities, and chances to grow in their abilities. See if these volunteers wish to be discipled by you or another church leader, then make that happen.

- *Deliberately include them in information loops.* Few things are as demotivating as working in an information vacuum. You want your ministry to be a place where the right hand *does* know what the left hand is doing. The first time your volunteer assigns people to do a task that turns out to be irrelevant, motivation sinks through the floor.

- *Provide stress release activities.* A movie ticket (or two, with an offer to have someone provide babysitting so the volunteer can take a spouse out on a date). Or if your budget is thin, a bag of microwave popcorn and gift certificate for a video rental. You'll have to find out what each volunteer enjoys (A pass to the zoo? A prepaid game of bowling? A magazine gift subscription?) to make a personal gift, but that's the point: You took the time to find out. And you appreciate that the volunteer is making a significant contribution.

Medium Responsibility Volunteer Jobs

These people are often implementing fairly defined tasks. They don't supervise other volunteers but may supervise a function—this is the volunteer who keeps the lawn mowed all summer, or who keeps the kitchen organized. That function is their responsibility.

Ways to encourage people in this sort of position include . . .

- *Help the volunteer hone his or her skills.* You honor the volunteer and the importance of what the volunteer is doing when you say, "Great job keeping the grounds looking sharp. Here's a subscription to a magazine that's all about lawn care, or a ticket to a lawn care show at the civic center."

- *Join the volunteer and ask for a demonstration.* Especially if the volunteer works alone, having some company will be welcome. Plus, showing up and asking questions is affirming.

Low Responsibility Volunteer Jobs

The duties performed by these volunteers are clearly defined and specific. Often, these positions are the "bite-sized" commitments that last either for a short time, or that are seemingly unimportant.

Ways to encourage people in this sort of position include . . .

- *Make sure they know they're important!* If at all possible, have the pastor or another recognizable church leader sign letters of thanks to these volunteers. Even better: Ask the pastor to walk through the church some Sunday thanking the nursery workers, greeters, and parking lot attendants who are often overlooked.

- *Give the worker a gift that connects his or her volunteer job to the larger church mission.* Making the connection is critical. If the volunteer is a parking lot attendant, give him or her a keychain. If the person is a greeter, give her a welcome mat for her home and thank her for making the church a welcoming place.

Constantly Improve Your Encouragement-Giving Skills

That was a good start on creative, practical recognition ideas, but more important than your doing lots of encouraging things is your becoming a consistently encouraging person. Hone your encouragement-giving skills until encouragement flows out of you naturally.

> "Encouragement is infectious; it spreads quickly."

Encouragement is infectious; it spreads quickly. But somebody has to get it started. Let it be you!

If you're not convinced that an encouraging spirit (accompanied by encouraging actions) is a crucial piece of volunteer-managing character equipment, then just open your Bible. You'll find countless examples of encouragement coming not only from Jesus and other leaders, but from other believers. Consider these passages . . .

> *I long to see you so that I may impart to you some spiritual gift to make you strong—that is, that you and I may be mutually encouraged by each other's faith. (Romans 1:11-12)*

> *Therefore encourage each other with these words. . . . Therefore encourage one another and build each other up, just as in fact you are doing. (1 Thessalonians 4:18; 5:11)*

> *Encourage one another daily, as long as it is called Today, so that none of you may be hardened by sin's deceitfulness. (Hebrews 3:13)*

> *Let us consider how we may spur one another on toward love and good deeds. Let us not give up meeting together, as some are in the habit of doing, but let us encourage one another —and all the more as you see the Day approaching. (Hebrews 10:24-25)*

Fill your ministry with encouragement and recognition and you'll create a culture that's fair . . . forgiving . . . and fun! That's how it's been for me, and I know it will be the same for you.

Volunteers are wonderful people. They're choosing to give of themselves and their time to serve others. But that alone doesn't take away the very real, very legitimate needs they have in their own lives. With your guidance, the volunteer ministry can help meet many of your volunteers' needs even as they're serving others. And there's nothing more encouraging than having your needs met!

Volunteers are people, and as people they have a desire to belong someplace where they are appreciated and valued. You can provide that.

They want to know their opinions matter. As you listen deeply, you'll provide that.

They want to give themselves to something bigger than themselves. As you connect them with appropriate volunteer positions in the church, you'll help them serve in the kingdom of God.

They want to be challenged, to grow, to become excellent in doing things that matter. The volunteer positions you'll help them find and the training you'll help them receive will let that happen.

The encouragement that comes from participating in the volunteer ministry is more than a passing "feel-good" experience. You're more than a cheerleader who rallies the troops. What happens in a volunteer's heart can be a life-changing experience. It can build new skills, rekindle old passions for service, and encourage lasting relationships—including a relationship with Jesus Christ and his church.

1. The content of this chapter draws heavily from Betty Stallings' Volunteer Management Program video presentation, *Recognition: Letting People Know You Noticed*. Betty B. Stallings is a premier trainer, consultant, and author specializing in volunteerism, nonprofit fundraising, board development, and leadership. She can be reached at 1717 Courtney Avenue, Pleasanton, CA 94588.

2. The chart "Recognition Based on Motivational Type" is from Betty B. Stallings.

SIX
What I Still Believe

Wise words and encouragement—for you.

I was asked to close this series on Volunteer Leadership with some "wisdom, insights, and inspiration." This challenge got me thinking about the concept of wisdom, and led me to revisit one of my favorite quotes from T. S. Eliot:

> "Where is the life we have lost in living?
> "Where is the wisdom we have lost in knowledge?
> "Where is the knowledge we have lost in information?"

–T.S. Eliot, *The Complete Poems and Plays 1909-1950*, Copyright 1971 by Esme Valerie Eliot (New York: Harcourt, Brace & World, Inc.), p.96.

Pondering the idea of wisdom, and reflecting on this quote, I decided these are the things I believe about wisdom:

• Wisdom deals with the "why" questions; knowledge and information deal with the "what and how."

• Wisdom deals with future implications; knowledge and information tend to concentrate on the present.

• Wisdom deals with principles and values (paradigms); knowledge and information deal with practices.

• Wisdom seeks to understand the questions; knowledge and information look for the answers.

• Wisdom is going deeper; knowledge and information tend to just keep getting broader.

Wisdom deals with the "whys" of what we do, with the future implications of our decisions, and with the principles and values underlying our decisions and practices. Wisdom calls us to be willing to ask hard questions that move us deeper into the meaning of what we do.

It's not that knowledge and information aren't important! They're essential in helping us reshape, re-form, and innovate our practices in the field of volunteer leadership. Knowledge and information keep us viable and appropriate. That's why this series is devoted to the practical, day-to-day "how-to's."

But I find an intriguing tension between knowledge/information and wisdom. As I pondered this, it became clear to me; it is often the challenge of what to let go of—and what to hold fast to—in the midst of all the changes. As T. S. Eliot also said:

> "We shall not cease from exploration, and the end of all exploring will be to arrive where we started—and know the place for the first time."

–T.S. Eliot, *The Complete Poems and Plays 1909-1950*, p.145.

I want to share with you some powerful principles that have stood the test of time through more than 35 years of my writing, teaching, and doing volunteer leadership in churches and nonprofit settings. They're what I still believe after all this time about leadership, management, volunteerism, and groups.

Thankfully, I know these principles in a new way (for the first time!) from the vantage point of age and experience. The years have certainly brought about change in what I know—the "how-to's"—but the principles stand.

I share these principles with you, knowing that the real value isn't what I'm writing here. Rather, I hope it will encourage you to make your own list!

My Powerful Principles

1. Volunteers are priceless.

I have a strong, foundational belief about volunteers that undergirds and fuels all the work I've done through the years. I can sum up this belief in a simple line I heard more than 30 years ago:

"Volunteers are not paid—not because they're worthless, but because they're priceless!"

Contrast that attitude toward volunteers with others you may have witnessed:

"Volunteers are nice, but not necessary."

"Volunteers are more work than they're worth."

"They're okay, as long as they don't cost us anything."

"We'll use them to save money, but they should be seen and not heard."

The attitudes of your church leadership toward volunteers permeates your church and has a dramatic effect on how volunteers feel about serving there. I believe in volunteers. I urge you to do the same.

2. People must be as important as programs, products, or profits.

The truth is that leaders either grow or diminish those who work with them. So if we meet our goals at the expense of the health, well-being, and growth of our people, we've ultimately failed. Everything we do in a volunteer ministries program must be grounded in these basics of theology:

• The priesthood of all believers

• The whole body of Christ

• The giftedness of each child of God

Revisit volume 1 of this Volunteer Leadership Series regularly to let these theological truths sink deep into your thinking and values. We haven't always embraced these theologies. For example, in the 1950s many churches focused on creating excellent programs. We decided to only let those who were excellent singers sing . . . only the excellent musicians could play during worship services . . . and we lost people who weren't professional performers.

In the 1990s corporations focused so much on products

and profits that they sometimes worked people literally to death—at least the death of their marriages.

People are important, too. They're designed for eternity.

3. People become committed to plans they help make. So plan *with*, not *for*, people.

This idea has gone through several fads and phases over the years, such as: "participative management" and "quality circles." Organizations spent millions bringing in gurus to teach them how to do planning . . . but many organizations never caught *why* planning with people makes sense.

It makes sense because the real wisdom is in the group itself. That's where the corporate genius resides, as well as the motivation to see plans succeed.

Far too often it became a gimmick to manipulate groups, and that always failed. People are too smart for this!

Stephen Covey observed, "It simply makes no difference how good the rhetoric is, or even how good the intentions are. If there is little or no trust, there is no foundation for permanent success. Only basic goodness gives life to techniques."[1]

4. Mission motivates; maintenance does not.

That's why one of your primary tasks is casting the vision, then keeping it alive.

Vision must be tied to tasks—that provides action.

Action must be tied to vision—that provides purpose and meaning.

Vision alone isn't enough. Action alone isn't enough.

Make sure everyone who works with you—volunteers and staff—knows your mission and how their work makes it happen.

5. Integrity and trust are the leader's most powerful assets; they have to be carefully and patiently earned.

If this is true, then the foundation for all team building is three-pronged: truth, trust, and clear expectations.

6. You must care for and tend your teams.

As go your teams, so goes your ministry. Watch carefully, so you know how a team is developing. You may see . . .

A *Parasitic* Team (competitive) where 1 + 1 = less than two.
A *Symbiotic* Team (cooperative) where 1 + 1 = 2.
A *Synergistic* Team (collaborative) where 1 + 1 = 3.

Grow healthy teams that move toward synergy. It's so simple—but so often overlooked because of expediency.

7. **Avoid the trap of becoming either a specialist or a generalist.**

A specialist is someone who knows more and more about less and less, until they know practically everything about almost nothing. A generalist is someone who knows less and less about more and more until they know almost nothing about everything.

8. **Be yourself—no one else is better qualified.**

In other words, be true to your principles and not swayed by fad or fashion. There is no substitute for being congruent in what you say and what you do—it builds trust in others and gives you peace of mind. For example, be sure to use volunteers yourself. It's what gives you credibility and makes you an effective advocate for volunteerism.

9. **The key to wise leadership is effective delegation, and the key to delegation (and motivation) is getting the right people in the right jobs.**

May I share a tip with you that has served me well for many years? Do not only accept—but actually seek out someone who knows more than you do where you need help. Then let them do the job—and be glad they succeed!

How do you get the right people in the right jobs? Know them by talking to them (interviewing) and observing them in action. Watch when their eyes light up. McClelland's Theory of Motivation of achievers, affiliators, and power people has been incredibly helpful to me here.

10. **Motivating others is critical to your success.**

I believe what John Gardner said about motivation: "Leaders do not create motivation . . . they unlock or channel existing motives."[2]

Let your own enthusiasm, excitement, and dedication to your mission shine through your work—it's contagious! My late husband, Harvey, used to say to me, "You love what you do so much—you don't even know it's work." How blessed I've been.

12. To become advocates and innovators, develop these three C's in your life: curiosity, creativity, and courage.

With those qualities in your life, be alert to identify problems and challenges that "have your name on them" (because of your past experience and skill), and take ownership of them.

Don't worry about knowing how to solve the problems; figuring it out is the fun part. And you don't need to know how it will all turn out. Just step up to the plate and take on issues when it's time to engage; let go when it's time to let go.

13. I can't help others if I don't stay well myself. So take care of me!

In this world it's often a great challenge to survive. But plants survive. Dogs and cats survive. I want to live embracing life with empathy and a zeal borne out of passion. That's living . . . and that's my goal.

I've heard it said that each of us is a house with four rooms—physical, mental, emotional, and spiritual. Most of us tend to live in one room most of the time. But unless we go into every room every day, even if only to keep it aired out, we're not complete people. What a vivid metaphor for health and wholeness! If you're serious about staying well, you will find time to:

> **Do the necessary housecleaning to rid your rooms of clutter and toxic waste.** This means "letting go" of lots of stuff! (You can't stumble on things that are behind you.)

> **Know your own needs.** If you can't name your own needs, then you don't deserve to have them met.

> **Be sure to not only visit each of your rooms every day, but slowly and lovingly furnish those rooms with things that nourish you, replenish you, and**

give you joy. No one can do that for you. We need to be the caretakers of our own lives.

14. It's important to keep the soul in our work.

Wayne Muller tells the story of a South American tribe that would go on long marches, day after day. All of a sudden they would stop walking, sit down, rest, and then make camp for a couple of days. They explained that they needed the time to rest so that their souls could catch up with them.[3] A concept I love.

My hope for you is that you'll rise to the challenges in volunteer ministry with clear vision, a list of your own powerful principles, new and creative "how to's," and all the energy, enthusiasm, dedication, joy . . . and yes, *soul*, you have! That you have the wisdom to determine what to keep, what to change, what to drop—and what to create.

To do this you'll need the courage of pioneers, the ingenuity of entrepreneurs, the enthusiasm and fearlessness of five-year-olds, the dedication and compassion of volunteers, and the wisdom of Solomon.

One final thing: You'll need the firm faith that nothing worthwhile is ever impossible with God's help.

1: Stephen Covey, *7 Habits of Highly Effective People* (New York: Simon and Schuster, 1989), p. 21.

2. John Gardner, *On Leadership* (New York: The Free Press, A Division of Macmillan, Inc., 1990).

3. Wayne Muller, *Sabbath: Restoring the Sacred Rhythm of Rest* (New York: Bantam Book, 1999), p. 70.

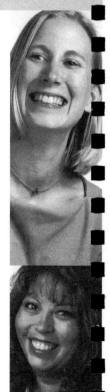
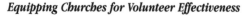